43 Ways to Finance
Your Feature Film

D0958919

43 Ways
to Finance
Your Feature Film

A Comprehensive Analysis of Film Finance

Updated Edition

John W. Cones

Southern Illinois University Press
Carbondale and Edwardsville

Library of Congress Cataloging-in-Publication Data

Cones, John W.
    43 ways to finance your feature film : a comprehensive analysis of
film finance / John W. Cones. — Updated ed.
        p.   cm.
    Includes bibliographical references and index.
    1. Motion pictures—Finance. I. Title.
    PN1993.5.A1C64   1998
    384′.83—dc21   97-50007
    ISBN 0-8093-2202-1 (pbk. : alk. paper)   CIP

The paper used in this publication meets the minimum requirements of
American National Standard for Information Sciences—Permanence of
Paper for Printed Library Materials, ANSI Z39.48-1984. ⊗

For all of those struggling independent producers
who deserve to have the information
contained in this book

CONTENTS

PASSIVE INVESTOR (SECURITIES) VEHICLES

PART 4: Foreign Financing

ACKNOWLEDGMENTS

An early draft of this book was used as one of two texts and as a basis for discussion in the author's fall 1993 class on independent feature film financing and distribution at the graduate-level Independent Producers Program, University of California at Los Angeles, and in a lecture on film finance and distribution for the University of Southern California School of Cinema-Television. Graduate and undergraduate students in the respective schools' writing, directing, producing, business and law programs attending those classes provided useful comments for the book.

An early draft of the book was also utilized as part of the seminar handouts for one of the author's two-day weekend seminars held on November 6 and 7, 1993, in Boise, Idaho, under the sponsorship of the Idaho Department of Commerce, the Idaho Film and Video Association and the Idaho Small Business Development Center. Certain of the filmmakers, attorneys, accountants, broker/dealers, film commissioners, film students, government officials and others in attendance at that gathering also contributed useful comments that were incorporated in the final version of the book.

INTRODUCTION

Presumably all books are written to meet a perceived need, preferably a perceived need in the target audience for the information presented in the book. This book was written for that same reason, that is, to meet a need within the American film industry for an objective and balanced overview of information relating to the numerous film-financing options and their respective advantages and disadvantages. The book is for those people, whether they are producers, executive producers, attorneys, screenwriters, investors or others, who are thinking about making or investing in a feature film and trying to determine the best way to go about financing the production costs of their films.

The need exists for two reasons: (1) each year in the United States, thousands of people are confronted with the question, How can I finance the costs of producing my feature film? and (2) none of the currently available books, articles or seminar presentations provide a comprehensive overview of the subject.

Production money financing for feature films. The focus of this book is on film finance, primarily for feature films as opposed to short films, documentaries, videos and other types of entertainment or informational projects, although much of the information presented will be useful in financing those kinds of projects as well. The book further focuses on what is involved in raising the money to pay for the costs associated with the production of such films as opposed to either development or distribution costs, although, again, much of what is discussed in this book may apply to either of those film-financing topics, depending on the type of financing chosen.

Film finance versus distribution. As a practical matter, it is impossible and even misleading to attempt to discuss film finance without also discussing certain aspects of film distribution, that is, those aspects that help to determine how revenues generated from the exploitation of a motion picture in all markets and media flow back to the owners, contingent compensation participants, financiers and/or investors. Nevertheless, this book will strive to emphasize as much as possible the front side of the transaction (film finance) instead of the back side (financial aspects of film distribution) and keep references to distribution to a minimum.

An overview. This book also does not attempt to provide an in-depth discussion of each of the forms of film finance covered. If in-depth coverage were the goal, at least four books would be needed to adequately cover the main areas of film finance: (1) studio/industry financing, (2) lender financing, (3) investor financing and (4) foreign financing. For that reason, each chapter of this volume provides numerous suggestions for further reading so that readers who are interested in a particular form of film finance can easily find additional and more complete information on that topic.

Comprehensive but not exhaustive. Although this book may present a discussion of more forms of film finance than any preceding effort relating to the topic, it still does not cover all forms of film finance. For example, in the area of investor financing, there are numerous other possibilities including general partnerships, that is, unincorporated associations of two or more persons doing business as co-owners for profit. Some feature film production companies operate as general partnerships, and a domestic coproduction may be classified as a general partnership, although more likely as a joint venture, which is covered in this book.

Other investor forms of film finance include the original nonpublic securities offering exemption, Section 4(2) of the 1933 Securities Act, along with Section 4(6) for use when sales are being made exclusively to accredited investors. Since Regulation D has generally replaced those earlier federal exemptions, they are not covered in this book. Some might further suggest inclusion of Section 3(a)(11) of the 1933 Securities Act (the intrastate exemption), but its use is really designed for truly local situations, that is, when most of the money is raised, spent and earned within one state. On the other hand, feature films may be shot anywhere and are intended to be exploited in markets and media throughout the world.

It is also true that the so-called back-door offering has actually been used by privately held film production companies as a way to go public, but that form of film finance is not included here. For example, the Samuel Goldwyn Company absorbed an already existing public company (the American Stock Exchange company, Heritage Entertainment, Inc.) in a Chapter 11 bankruptcy reorganization and emerged as a publicly traded company in the early nineties. That particular type of transaction is viewed as a bit too exotic even for this presentation, and numerous other sophisticated corporate securities transactions have also been omitted for that same reason.

In addition, feature films have been financed from time to time with grant monies, more specifically, several grants in combination and through not-for-profit organizations. The omission of a chapter on grants and not-for-profits does not suggest that grant funding is not a viable form of film finance, in some circumstances, but merely reflects an editorial decision not to include a chapter on that topic because of the constraints of time and space.

Others who lecture on film finance sometimes talk about friend/family financing, weekend filmmaking, self-financing, student filmmaking, credit card financing or other versions of the same themes, and even though it is possible to create useful material relating to such topics, they were not deemed significant enough to be included in this presentation.

Why forty-three? The choice of forty-three is somewhat arbitrary. A number smaller or larger (as pointed out above) could have been chosen. A book on various forms of film finance could have been presented as the "Four Major Types of Film Finance" as described above in the paragraph "An Overview." Other forms of film finance actually described in this book are not truly stand-alone financing methods, for example, "business plans" (chapter 15) and "talent agency financing" (chapter 7). Still others could have been covered in one chapter, for example, all three of the specific securities exemptions under Regulation D. It just so happens that forty-three was the author's original estimate of the number of forms of film finance that could be reasonably discussed in a book of this nature, and although during the actual writing of the book, various editorial decisions were made—splitting, combining, adding and/or omitting chapters—the forty-three stayed on as a comfortable number.

Availability analysis. Finally, a book that focuses on providing an analysis of the advantages and disadvantages of various forms of film finance, as this one does, may necessarily have to overlook one of the most important advantages or disadvantages, as the case may be, if it does not discuss the *availability* of such forms of film finance, that is, the question as to whether a particular form of film finance is realistically available in the marketplace for a particular filmmaker on a particular project at a given time, regardless of what other advantages attract the filmmaker to that form of film finance. Unfortunately, differing forms of film finance are more or less available to different people, depending on the specific project, its budget, other film elements, along with the relationships and other resources that such persons bring to the table, and so forth. In addition, reliable *availability* information is difficult to come by in the film industry, if for no other reason than there is no organization that routinely develops and makes objective, comprehensive film-financing information available to those who need it. Thus, before ultimately determining which form of film finance is best for a particular film project at a given time, the reader should first attempt to objectively analyze whether that form of film finance is realistically available for that person, that project and at that particular moment.

The industry critic. From time to time, some cynicism about the film industry will creep into the analysis presented in this book, stemming from, at the very least, a general feeling held by the author and many others who have long worked in the film industry that all is not right with this business of film. For example, if it is true that the American feature film industry is an "insider's game"[1] and a "relationship-driven business"[2] whose inside players rely heavily on an ongoing series of "reciprocal preference transactions,"[3] nepotism[4] and other forms of discrimination, then those high-level issues certainly will have an impact on anybody's objective analysis of the advantages and disadvantages of various forms of film finance. Thus, some mention of such real-world considerations will be included where appropriate in this book.

This book is published with the understanding that the author is not herein engaged in rendering legal, accounting or other professional services. If legal advice or other expert assistance is required, the services of a professional person should be engaged for that specific purpose. All opinions expressed in this book are those of the author.

1. See "Piercing Indictment" by Steven Gaydos, *Los Angeles Reader*, December 11, 1992.
2. See *Reel Power* by Mark Litwak (William Morrow, 1986), 160.
3. See "The Recent Acquisition of Theatre Circuits by Major Distributors" by Gerald F. Phillips, *The Entertainment and Sports Lawyer* 5, no. 3 (Winter 1987): 13.
4. See "Hollywood's Family Ways" by Terry Pristin, Calendar section of *Los Angeles Times*, January 31, 1993.

PART 1

Industry Financing

1

Studio Development and In-House Production Deals

One of the first ways a film producer might consider financing a film project is to enter the so-called studio system at the earliest opportunity, that is, at the acquisition/development stage of a film project. The term *development* refers to the initial stage in the preparation of a film. Development comprises those activities relating specifically to taking a concept or idea and turning it into a finished screenplay. Development involves formulating and organizing the concept or idea for the movie; acquiring rights to the underlying literary work or screenplay; preparing an outline, synopsis and/or treatment; and writing, polishing and revising the various drafts of the script.

The studio in-house production usually starts as a development deal either initiated by a writer, director or producer or by the studio with one or more of such persons. The development deal typically begins with the pitching of an idea or film concept to a studio creative executive and/or the submission of a synopsis, treatment, outline or draft screenplay to the creative department of the studio. Regardless of who claims ownership of the original motion picture concept, if the studio finances the development of the screenplay, the production of the movie and its distribution expenses, the studio will ultimately own most, if not all, rights associated with the project.

Committing to production. A major studio/distributor will generally not commit itself to the production financing for a motion picture until a substantially developed package exists (i.e., at least a first draft of a screenplay is completed, a budget has been prepared and a director and actors have been attached to the project).

The step deal. A studio development deal is generally referred to as a Step Deal because the development financing is handled in stages, that is, the studio will pay the producer and other persons who are contributing to the property's development (e.g., writer and di-

3

rector) a salary, and sometimes expense money, in increments as the project is developed. The first step might involve developing an outline of the screenplay; the second step might involve developing a first draft of the script and so forth. The studio will have the right to decline to develop the project beyond any given stage, if it so chooses.

Office on the lot. Some deals are nothing more than handshake arrangements between a producer and a studio executive in which the producer is provided with office space on the lot in exchange for a *first look* at whatever projects are developed by the producer. Having an office on a studio lot gives the producer a certain level of credibility, which in turn presumably helps him or her acquire, develop and package projects. Other office-on-the-lot arrangements are more extensive (see chapter 3).

The development deal memo. Typically, the development deal is first memorialized in writing by means of a deal memo, which is just an abbreviated version of a more formal written agreement (usually, for example, in letter form). It outlines the basic *deal points* (terms) of the agreement, such as salary, time schedules, screen credit and percentage participation in the film's profits. The more formal contract containing the details of the agreement is negotiated and prepared by agents and/or attorneys while the project is in active development. That agreement may be referred to as an Executive Producer Agreement, a Producer's Agreement, a Director's Agreement or a Writer's Agreement, depending on with whom the development deal is made.

Producer's salary. The salary that the producer negotiates for the development deal is typically the entire salary such producer will receive if and when the movie is actually produced. That figure may be a significant and an enticing amount of money, but the producer must keep in mind that getting the entire amount is highly speculative, because of the nature of the development process, the unfavorable odds of actually going into production and the fact that the studio can stop the process at any stage. Only a small portion of that total salary is usually paid during the actual development process.

Advantages

Studio money. The writer, director, producer or executive producer who goes to the studio is not usually required to put up any of his or her money to finance the development, production or distribution of the film, although without a track record and/or relationship with the studio some acquisition costs may have to be incurred by the producer.

Major motion picture. In the current motion picture marketplace, the major studio/distributors dominate in the area of theatrical releases. Thus, if anyone associated with a particular film project wants the film to be a so-called major motion picture, it will, as a practical matter, have to be developed, produced and/or at least released by a major studio/distributor.

Insider development companies. Certain production/development companies whose owners have strong relationships with studio insiders have the best shot at getting studio development deals and may be able to make good money developing film projects for studios, at least for a while, even if few or any of their projects are ever "green-lighted" for production.

Bigger pictures. A studio can generally provide more significant resources to aid in the development of a project, that is, can offer the promise of a higher production budget and the ability to obtain commitments from the bigger name stars at an earlier stage, than other available development financing sources.

Collaborative process. In some instances, the extensive collaborative process that studios engage in through the development and production of a motion picture (e.g., using several different writers, a producer, a director and studio executives, all contributing ideas during development) actually results in an improved version of the film. On the other hand, not all collaborators are equals in this process.

Disadvantages

Not good odds. The odds against getting an idea, concept, synopsis, treatment, outline or script submitted to a studio and accepted as a development deal (much less given a green light for production) are tremendous. Major studios receive hundreds of submissions a week and thousands a year, only to choose a hundred or so for development and a handful for production.

Relationship-driven business. If all other things are approximately equal, the studio development or production green light will go to the producer who has the best relationship with the studio or the studio executives making the commitment on behalf of the studio. Some in the industry characterize this phenomenon as studio politics or refer to the industry as a relationship-driven business. This is also one of the situations in which Hollywood nepotism, favoritism and cronyism come into play.

Danger of theft. It is very difficult for industry outsiders to protect against theft of ideas, or even the tangible expression of those ideas, while trying to interest a studio, production company or distributor in a film project. The copyright laws provide inadequate protection for writers in this environment.

Fewer deals available. The major studio/distributors appear to have cut back in recent years on the number of development deals they will accept.

An insider's game. Studio financing at the development or production stage appears to be pretty much an insider's game; thus, if an independent producer does not have a relationship with a studio executive, the chances of obtaining a development deal are even less likely. Merit does not always win in Hollywood.

Development hell. Sometimes a film project in development at a studio just never seems to get a green light for production but remains in development for what seems like an eternity. This is often referred to as "development hell."

Turnaround. In some cases, producers may have a difficult time regaining ownership of the original property if it never receives a "go" to production and is placed in *turnaround* by the studio. Producers should insist on putting a time limit on turnaround.

Producer's fee only. Only a few very powerful persons ever obtain a significant and meaningful participation in the upside potential of a studio in-house production that started out as the project of such an individual.

Not adequately developed. Sometimes movies developed by studios are needed to fill the studio/distributor's release slots for a given year and are prematurely committed to production to meet those needs even though the film projects are not adequately developed.

Bumped by agency projects. Film projects in development at a studio may get replaced by fully packaged projects brought to the studio by a powerful talent agency.

Studio employee. A person submitting a project to a studio for development in effect becomes an employee of the studio and may not only lose control of the project but may be fired under some circumstances.

Further Reading

Adventures in the Screen Trade. William Goldman. Warner Books, 1983.

"Box Office Champions." Paul Kagan. Paul Kagan Associates (updated annually).

Copyright Registration Practice. James E. Hawes. Clark Boardman Callaghan, 1990.

Entertainment, Publishing and the Arts Handbook. Edited by Michael Meyer and John David Viera. Clark Boardman, 1984.

Film and Video Financing. Michael Wiese. Michael Wiese Productions, 1991.

Film Finance and Distribution—A Dictionary of Terms. John W. Cones. Silman-James Press, 1992.

Film Industry Contracts. John W. Cones. Self-published, 1993.

"Film Producers, Studios, Agents and Casting Directors" (directory). Lone Eagle Publishing (updated periodically).

The Films of the Eighties: A Social History. William J. Palmer. Southern Illinois University Press, 1993.

Financing Your Film. Trisha Curran. Praeger Publishers, 1986.

Framing Blackness—The African American Image in Film. Ed Guerrero. Temple University Press, 1993.

The Hollywood Reporter Blu-Book. Published annually by *The Hollywood Reporter*.

Independent Feature Film Production—A Complete Guide from Concept to Distribution. Gregory Goodell. St. Martin's Press, 1982.

Law and Business of the Entertainment Industries. 2d ed. Donald E. Biederman, Edward P. Pierson, Martin E. Silfen, Jeanne A. Glasser, and Robert C. Berry. Praeger Publishers, 1991.

Making Money in Film and Video. 2d ed. Raul daSilva. Focal Press, 1992.

"Masters of the Deal." Cameron Stauth. *American Film*, May 1991.

Motion Picture Marketing and Distribution. Fred Goldberg. Focal Press, 1991.

"Net Profit Participations in the Motion Picture Industry." Hillary Bibicoff. *Loyola Entertainment Law Journal* 11 (1991).

Never Enough: The "A" Deal, Business, Legal and Ethical Realities. Sixteenth Annual UCLA Entertainment Symposium, February 1992 (annual symposium publication).

Producing, Financing and Distributing Film: A Comprehensive Legal and Business Guide. 2d ed. Paul A. Baumgarten, Donald C. Farber, and Mark Fleischer. Limelight Editions, 1992.

"Structuring Film Development Deals." Marc Jacobson. *Entertainment Law and Finance*, September 1990.

"Successful Producing in the Entertainment Industry" (seminar). Mark Litwak. UCLA Extension, 1990.

They Can Kill You But They Can't Eat You . . . and Other Lessons from the Front. Dawn Steel. Simon and Schuster's Pocket Books, 1993.

What a Producer Does. Buck Houghton. American Film Institute, 1991.

"Why Savvy Independents are 'Cocooning' with the Major Studios." Robert Marich. *The Hollywood Reporter Entertainment Financing Special Report*, p. S-8, January 1991.

Women and Film—A Sight and Sound Reader. Foreword by Phillip Dodd. Temple University Press, 1993.

2

The Studio Production-Financing/ Distribution Deal

In contrast to the studio in-house production, the studio production-financing/distribution deal generally starts with the submission of a partially or fully packaged film project including a fairly well developed screenplay. In other words, the development phase of the screenplay is substantially complete. Thus, there is no longer any need for a development deal. The packaged film project is brought in to the studio by an independent producer who has already incurred the acquisition and development costs or through a talent agency with or without a producer attached.

Package. A film package minimally consists of a script, a budget, a shooting schedule and often commitments by a star or stars and a director. It can also be enhanced by including deferments from a film laboratory, performers or director and having part of the production funding already raised or committed. Some agents, agencies, entertainment attorneys and others engage in packaging activities and use several of their own clients in the same film project. Those transactions are at least partly motivated by the desire to maximize the agent's or attorney's fees.

Production-financing/distribution agreement. The P-F/D agreement is a contract between the studio/distributor (or other distributor) and a feature film producer that sets out the terms and conditions under which the distributor will provide production financing for a motion picture in exchange for the right to distribute the film in some or all markets. The P-F/D arrangement is one of the principal forms of motion picture production financing.

With the P-F/D deal, the studio assumes the role of the lender in the transaction and actually lends the production money to the production entity. In addition, the studio's affiliated distribution arm handles distribution for the completed picture.

Studio approvals. The items over which a major studio/distribu-

9

tor has the right to approve or disapprove in the context of a feature film P-F/D agreement are referred to as "studio approvals." As a general rule, the more money a producer tries to get from a studio, the more approvals a studio is likely to impose. Such approvals typically relate to the screenplay, budget, producer, director, lead performers, start date, running time, Motion Picture Association of America (MPAA) rating, locations and production schedule.

Takeover rights. Typically, the production-financing/distribution agreement will provide that the studio/distributor has the right to take over production of the motion picture if the cost of producing the film has exceeded a certain specified percentage of the budget (for example, 10 percent) or if the production has fallen behind schedule by a certain number of days.

Form of film finance sought. When approaching a major studio/distributor or other potential industry funding source, it is important for the producer to have some idea which form of film finance he or she is seeking and what the basic advantages and disadvantages are for each. This helps to make the producer's discussions with the potential funding source more meaningful. Thus, with a major studio/distributor it is important to know whether the producer is seeking a development deal, a production-financing/distribution agreement, a negative pickup or merely talking with the distribution division about a possible future acquisition of an independently financed film. In many instances, those choices help to determine which of the studio employees actually meet and talk with the producer.

Advantages

Big-budget films. A high-budget feature film developed by an independent producer outside the studio system may have to be produced under a P-F/D arrangement since the major studio/distributors are generally the only entities in a position to accept or control the financial risks involved.

Expensive talent. Many of the high salaries demanded by agents on behalf of their top director, actor and actress clients can only be underwritten by the major studio/distributors who are generally in the best position to make judgments about the financial prospects for a given film.

Producer advances. Producer advances are likely to be larger in the P-F/D deal than in any other form of film finance.

Distribution treatment. The studio-financed motion picture is more likely to receive favorable treatment in distribution than non-studio releases, not necessarily because the films are better than other available releases, but because the major studio/distributors have greater economic power and leverage with the exhibitors.

Box office dominance. The major studio/distributor releases have provided the major studios with an approximate average market share of 92 percent of box office gross in the domestic theatrical marketplace in the last ten years or so.

Collections. The major studio/distributors also have greater leverage with the exhibitors when it comes time to collect distributor rentals. Thus, they are likely to be able to extract a higher percentage of the box office gross from the exhibitors.

Disadvantages

Creative Control. Distributors who put up some or all of the production money for a film will usually exercise extensive controls and approvals over the production process; thus, an independent producer relying on the P-F/D method of film finance may be giving up a significant amount of creative control.

Unconscionable agreements. P-F/D agreements are notoriously one-sided (in favor of the distributor). Thus, most producers or other net-profit or net-proceed participants have little, if any, chance of participating in the upside potential of a motion picture produced in this manner. It may, in fact, be fair to characterize most all of the major studio/distributor distribution deals as unconscionable or contracts of adhesion.

Settlement transactions. Notwithstanding the collections advantage of the major studio/distributor, the settlement transactions between the exhibitors and distributors clearly favor the studio-produced films as opposed to independently produced films, even those distributed by the major studio/distributors. In other words, certain of the exhibitors and distributors appear to be colluding to deprive the independent producer and all net- and gross-profit participants of such independently produced films from their profit participations when their films are distributed by the major studio/distributors. The settlement transaction between the exhibitors and distributors appears to be one of the principal mechanisms used to further such collusion.

Broad commercial appeal. Small films or low-budget films are generally not considered suitable for studio financing, using the P-F/D arrangement. Projects generally accepted for studio financing in this manner must at least appear to the studio executives to have a fairly broad commercial appeal, that is, appeal to the so-called lowest common denominator audience.

Higher interest rates. Interest rates charged by studios on P-F/D deals are generally higher than the rates charged by banks and other non-studio lenders who provide production-money financing for feature films.

Longer interest-paying period. Not only are the studio interest rates higher than the rates charged on bank loans, studio interest on a P-F/D loan is incurred during a longer period of time than in a bank-financed negative pickup deal since the studio-affiliated distributor generally first deducts its distribution fee, then recoups its distribution expenses, and then deducts interest incurred to date before ultimately recouping the negative cost of the picture.

Conflicts of interest. The inherent conflict of interest involved in packaging by entertainment attorneys or talent agents may result in a less than desirable combination of film elements that are presented to the studio, sometimes on a take-it-or-leave-it basis. When this occurs, the agent and the talent he or she represents, may benefit financially, but the studio, its stockholders, the movie-going audiences and the talent arbitrarily excluded from participation in the package are harmed.

Little chance of net profits. Profit participation auditors estimate that major studio/distributor releases generate net profits (or net proceeds) in only about 5 percent of the cases. Although this is merely an estimate, no one outside the studios is in a better position to make such estimates than profit participation auditors.

Less favorable terms for producers. As a general rule, the more financial risk a studio/distributor is asked to undertake in the production and distribution of a feature film, the more likely it is that the studio/distributor will extract more favorable terms for itself in the P-F/D agreement.

Overhead charges. The studio/distributor not only will deduct its distribution fee, distribution expenses, interest and the negative cost from the distributor gross receipts but will also generally include a specified percentage (usually 10 to 15 percent) of the negative cost of the motion picture as an overhead charge that is added to the negative cost and thus incurs additional interest.

Copyright ownership. A major studio/distributor that provides all of the production financing along with the distribution expenses for a feature film will in all likelihood insist on owning the copyrights to the film in addition to distributing the film throughout the universe in perpetuity. Thus, the picture becomes part of the studio/distributor's library of films as opposed to being an addition to the library of the independent producer.

Further Reading

Accounting Standards: Original Pronouncements. Financial Accounting Standards Board, 1983.

The American Movie Industry: The Business of Motion Pictures. G. Kindem. Southern Illinois University Press, 1982.

Anatomy of the Movies. David Pirie. McMillan, 1981.

Art Murphy's Box Office Register. Published annually by Art Murphy.

Box Office Champions. Paul Kagan. Paul Kagan Associates (updated annually).

"Buchwald v. Paramount Pictures Corp. and the Future of Net Profit." Adam J. Marcus. *Cardozo Arts & Entertainment Law Journal,* 9 (1991).

Communications Industry Survey. Veronis, Suhler and Associates (annual publication).

"Contingent Compensation for Theatrical Motion Pictures." David Nochimson and Leon Brachman. *The Entertainment and Sports Lawyer* 5, no. 1 (Summer 1986).

"Defining Net Profits, Shares for a Motion Picture Deal." Edward E. Colton. *New York Law Journal,* September 30, 1988.

Entertainment Industry Economics. 2d ed. Harold L. Vogel. Cambridge University Press, 1990.

Entertainment Law. Robert Fremlin. Clark Boardman Callaghan, 1991.

Entertainment Law. Melvin Simensky and Thomas Selz. Matthew Bender, 1984.

Entertainment Law: Legal Concepts and Business Practices. 2d ed. Thomas Selz, Melvin Simensky, and Patricia Acton. Shepard's, McGraw-Hill (updated periodically).

Fatal Subtraction—How Hollywood Really Does Business. Pierce O'Donnell and Dennis McDougal. Doubleday, 1992.

Film and Video Financing. Michael Wiese. Michael Wiese Productions, 1991.

Film Finance and Distribution—A Dictionary of Terms. John W. Cones. Silman-James Press, 1992.

Film Industry Contracts. John W. Cones. Self-published, 1993.

Film Producers, Studios, Agents and Casting Directors (directory). Lone Eagle Publishing (updated periodically).

The Films of the Eighties—A Social History. William J. Palmer. Southern Illinois University Press, 1993.

Final Cut. Steven Bach. William Morrow, 1982.

"Financing the Production of Theatrical Motion Pictures." Lionel S. Sobel. *Entertainment Law Reporter*, May 1984.

Framing Blackness—The African American Image in Film. Ed Guerrero. Temple University Press, 1993.

"Fundamental Aspects of U.S. Theatrical Film Biz." Art Murphy. *Daily Variety*, October 26, 1982.

Hollywood Be Thy Name: Random Recollections of a Movie Veteran from Silents to Talkies to TV. William Bakewell. Scarecrow Press.

The Hollywood Reporter Book of Box Office Hits. Susan Sackett. Billboard Books (updated periodically).

"Hollywood's Family Ways—Who Can You Trust Better Than Kin?" Terry Pristin. *Los Angeles Times* (Calendar section), January 31, 1993.

"How Hollywood Studios Flimflam Their Stars." F. Swertlow. *TV Guide*, May 1, 1982.

"How to Draft Multi-Picture Deals." Nigel Sinclair. *Entertainment Law and Finance*, January 1987.

"How to Negotiate Contracts, Deals in the Movie Industry." Edward E. Colton. *New York Law Journal*, September 23, 1988.

"Imagine There's No. . . . " Corie Brown. *Premiere*, p. 24, August 1992.

Indecent Exposure. David McClintock. William Morrow, 1982.

Independent Feature Film Production. Gregory Goodell. St. Martin's Press, 1982.

"In Hollywood's Jungle the Predators Are Out and Feasting on Stars." D. Akst and L. Landro. *Wall Street Journal*, June 20, 1988.

Intellectual Property and Antitrust Law. William C. Holmes. Clark Boardman Callaghan (updated periodically).

"It Didn't Begin with Begelman: A Concise History of Film Business Finagling." H. J. Salemson and M. Zolotow. *Action* (Director's Guild of America), July/August 1978.

I Wake Up Screening—Everything You Need to Know about Making Independent Films Including a Thousand Reasons Not To. Frank D. Gilroy. Southern Illinois University Press, 1993.

"Killing the Golden Goose: Hollywood's Death Wish." Pierce O'Donnell. *Beverly Hills Bar Journal*, Summer 1992.

Law and Business of the Entertainment Industries. 2d ed. Donald E. Biederman, Edward P. Pierson, Martin E. Silfen, Jeanne A. Glasser, and Robert C. Berry. Praeger Publishers, 1991.

"Lawyer Rips H'w'd, Calls for Reform." Kathleen O'Steen. *Daily Variety*, September 29, 1992.

"Majors Are Relying on Indies in a Major Way—Number of Outside Pix on Studios' Slates Is Rising." Lawrence Cohn. *Variety*, April 27, 1992.

Making Money in Film and Video. 2d ed. Raul daSilva. Focal Press, 1992.

"Masters of the Deal." Cameron Stauth. *American Film Magazine*, p. 28, May 1991.

Motion Picture Almanac. Quigley Publishing (annual publication).

The Motion Picture and Television Business. Entertainment Business Publishing (Beverly Hills, California), 1986.

Motion Picture Distribution: An Accountant's Perspective. David J. Leedy. Self-published, 1980.

Motion Picture Marketing and Distribution. Fred Goldberg. Focal Press, 1991.

The Movie Business Book. 2d ed. Edited by Jason E. Squire, A Fireside Book, 1992.

NATO Encyclopedia of Exhibition. National Association of Theatre Owners (annual publication).

"The Net Effect: Making Net Profit Mean Something." Peter J. Dekom. *American Premiere*, May-June 1992.

"Piercing Indictment—Accused of Trying to Destroy Tinseltown, Art Buchwald's Attorney Pleads 'Not Guilty' and Turns the Charges Back on his Accusers and You." Steven Gaydos. *Los Angeles Reader*, December 11, 1992.

Producing, Financing and Distributing Film—A Comprehensive Legal and Business Guide. 2d ed. Paul A. Baumgarten, Donald C. Farber, and Mark Fleischer. Limelight Editions, 1992.

"The Profit Participation Conundrum: A Glossary of Common Terms and Suggestions for Negotiation." Gunther H. Schiff. *Beverly Hills Bar Journal*, Summer 1992.

"Profit Participation in the Motion Picture Industry." Steven D. Sills and Ivan L. Axelrod. *Los Angeles Lawyer*, April 1989.

"Profits the Thing, Not the Box Office Tally—Top-Grossing Pix Don't Always Bring Biggest Returns." Lawrence Cohn. *Variety*, October 5, 1992.

"Projecting Profits from a Motion Picture" (excerpts from a self-published book). David J. Leedy. Lecture, UCLA Extension Class, "Contractual Aspects of Producing, Financing and Distributing Film," Fall 1991.

"Protecting Your Ideas in Hollywood." Lionel S. Sobel. *Writer's Friendly Legal Guide*. Writer's Digest Books, 1989.

Reel Power—The Struggle for Influence and Success in the New Hollywood. Mark Litwak. William Morrow, 1986.

Rolling Breaks, and Other Movie Business. Aljean Harmetz. Alfred A. Knopf, 1983.

"Rules of the Game—Between the Story Idea and the Movie Screen, There's a Long List of Executive No-No's." Jack Mathews. *American Film*, March 1990.

"Safe Harbor—In 1990s, Indies Quickly Discovering Best Lifeline Is Tied to a Major Distributor." Judy Brennan. *Daily Variety,* p. 12, June 26, 1991.

They Can Kill You But They Can't Eat You . . . and Other Lessons from the Front. Dawn Steel. Simon and Schuster's Pocket Books, 1993.

"Too Many Hoorays for Hollywood." William Cash. *The Spectator,* October 1992.

"Transition in the Motion Picture Industry—Financing and Distribution." Peter Dekom. *Counseling Clients in the Entertainment Industry.* Practicing Law Institute, 1984.

Understanding the Antitrust Laws. 9th ed. Jerrold G. Van Cise, William T. Lifland, and Laurence T. Sorkin. Practicing Law Institute, 1986.

What a Producer Does. Buck Houghton. American Film Institute, 1991.

"Why Savvy Independents are 'Cocooning' with the Major Studios." Robert Marich. *The Hollywood Reporter* Entertainment Financing Special Report, p. S-8, January 1991.

Women and Film—A Sight and Sound Reader. Foreword by Phillip Dodd. Temple University Press, 1993.

You'll Never Eat Lunch in This Town Again. Julia Phillips. Penguin Books, 1991.

3

Studio-based Independent Production Company Financing

Studio spokespersons report that each of the major studio/ distributor organizations (Warner Bros., Disney, SONY [Columbia and Tri-Star], Universal, Paramount, 20th Century Fox—a list that previously included MGM/UA and Orion, both of which may return to their respective levels of activity) have relationships with independent producers and their production companies, which typically include studio provision of offices on the studio lot. In turn, these producers have agreed to offer the studio a first look at whatever projects are developed by the independent producer (the so-called first-look deal). Each of the more active studios named above reportedly has about thirty to forty such relationships, which are also sometimes referred to as *housekeeping deals* or *overall deals*. Some industry-insider producers have been known to have a first-look deal at one studio, a next- or second-look deal at another studio, and a so-called third-look deal at still another major studio. After all, the studio executives who are making the commitments quite often shuffle back and forth between the major studios during their careers, creating the impression that such studio organizations really function as a single unit, particularly when it comes to competing with outsiders.

The studio contribution in one of the first-look deals may vary from a single no-frills office to a more elaborate complex of offices with secretaries, readers, office equipment and development financing. The producers were able to obtain these first-look deals presumably based on their reputations as feature film producers or on their relationships with the studio executives who are authorized to make such commitments on behalf of the studio. The associated development deals are presumably granted in conjunction with specific projects that have been pitched to the studio and accepted by the studio as projects under development (see chapter 1).

To research which companies have studio deals, see the *Holly-*

17

wood Creative Directory cited in the Further Reading section below. This directory provides a list of thirteen hundred production companies, studios, TV/cable networks; their addresses, phone numbers, faxes, produced credits and staff. In addition, it provides more than fifty-one hundred indexed and cross-referenced names of development and production personnel and their titles along with the names of companies and talent who have studio deals. The directory is published and updated every four months (March, July and November).

Advantages

Relationships in place. Independent producers seeking studio financing for their film projects may find that aligning themselves with other producers already on a lot will substantially increase their chances of getting their projects produced.

Using an intermediary. This strategy allows the independent producer to seek studio financing without placing so much emphasis on getting access to and developing a relationship with a studio executive but permits the possibility of studio financing by allowing another party who already has the relationship with the studio to become involved in the project.

The indirect approach. It may be easier to get a film produced by a studio going through one of the already established first-look deals than going directly to the studio. The studio executive may, in fact, ultimately refer the producer with an interesting project to one of the producers on the lot.

Fewer deals available. In recent years with the major studios under pressure to lower costs, fewer housekeeping deals have been offered.

Disadvantages

Nepotism, favoritism and cronyism. Unfortunately, many of these arrangements for providing independent producers with an office on the lot are awarded to family members or friends of family (see "Hollywood's Family Ways" cited below).

Special relationships. Some producers have even placed themselves in an obvious conflict-of-interest situation involving a loan or other form of inducement to a studio executive who may be in a position to grant an office-on-the-lot or production deal to that producer.

Thus, more ethical independent producers are at a clear disadvantage in getting the desired studio relationship.

Odds still not favorable. If in fact each of the major studios have some thirty to forty office-on-the-lot relationships with producers who are obligated in turn to provide the studio with a first look at the projects the producers develop, and the studios only release fifteen to twenty-four films a year (some of which have been produced completely outside the studio system), the odds of getting a green light on a feature production using this strategy are also discouraging.

The risk of inadvertent loss. The independent producer organizations that have relationships with the studios are often not very organized or well managed; thus, submitting a project to such a group can also result in loss of the project in other ways.

The development scam. Sometimes a producer submitting a developed screenplay to another producer on a studio lot is told that the project needs to be developed further and the producer on the lot then hires another writer to continue to develop the project, thus possibly creating an ownership interest in the project that might be ultimately used to squeeze out the original producer.

Further Reading

Box Office Champions. Paul Kagan. Paul Kagan Associates (updated annually).

"Buchwald v. Paramount Pictures Corp. and the Future of Net Profit." Adam J. Marcus. *Cardozo Arts & Entertainment Law Journal* 9 (1991).

"Contingent Compensation for Theatrical Motion Pictures." David Nochimson and Leon Brachman. *The Entertainment and Sports Lawyer* 5, no. 1 (Summer 1986).

"Defining Net Profits, Shares for a Motion Picture Deal." Edward E. Colton. *New York Law Journal*, September 30, 1988.

Entertainment Industry Economics. 2d ed. Harold L. Vogel. Cambridge University Press, 1990.

Entertainment Law. Melvin Simensky and Thomas Selz. Matthew Bender, 1984.

Entertainment Law: Legal Concepts and Business Practices. 2d ed. Thomas Selz, Melvin Simensky and Patricia Acton. Shepard's, McGraw-Hill (updated periodically).

"Every Trick in the Books." D. Wechsler. *Forbes*, May 29, 1989.

Fatal Subtraction—How Hollywood Really Does Business. Pierce O'Donnell and Dennis McDougal. Doubleday, 1992.

Film Finance and Distribution—A Dictionary of Terms. John W. Cones. Silman-James Press, 1992.

Film Industry Contracts. John W. Cones Self-published, 1993.

Film Producers, Studios, Agents and Casting Directors (directory). Lone Eagle Publishing (updated periodically).

"Financing the Production of Theatrical Motion Pictures." Lionel S. Sobel. *Entertainment Law Reporter,* May 1984.

Hollywood Creative Directory. Published by Hollywood Creative Directory (updated periodically).

"Hollywood's Bonfire of the Vanity Deals." Charles Fleming. *Variety,* p. 1, March 30, 1992.

"Hollywood's Family Ways—Who Can You Trust Better Than Kin?" Terry Pristin. *Los Angeles Times* (Calendar section), January 31, 1993.

"How to Draft Multi-Picture Deals." Nigel Sinclair. *Entertainment Law and Finance,* January 1987.

"How to Negotiate Contracts, Deals in the Movie Industry." Edward E. Colton. *New York Law Journal,* September 23, 1988.

Independent Feature Film Production. Gregory Goodell. St. Martin's Press, 1982.

"Killing the Golden Goose: Hollywood's Death Wish." Pierce O'Donnell. *Beverly Hills Bar Journal* (Summer 1992).

Law and Business of the Entertainment Industries. 2d ed. Donald E. Biederman, Edward P. Pierson, Martin E. Silfen, Jeanne A. Glasser and Robert C. Berry. Praeger Publishers, 1991.

"Lawyer Rips H'w'd, Calls for Reform." Kathleen O'Steen. *Daily Variety,* September 29, 1992.

"Low Budget." J. A. Trachtenberg. *Forbes,* March 26, 1984.

"Majors Are Relying on Indies in a Major Way—Number of Outside Pix on Studios' Slates Is Rising." Lawrence Cohn. *Variety,* April 27, 1992.

Making Money in Film and Video. 2d ed. Raul daSilva. Focal Press, 1992.

"Masters of the Deal." Cameron Stauth. *American Film Magazine,* p. 28, May 1991.

Motion Picture Marketing and Distribution. Fred Goldberg. Focal Press, 1991.

The Movie Business Book. 2d ed. Edited by Jason E. Squire. A Fireside Book, 1992.

"The Net Effect: Making Net Profit Mean Something." Peter J. Dekom. *American Premiere,* May-June, 1992.

"Piercing Indictment—Accused of Trying to Destroy Tinseltown, Art Buchwald's Attorney Pleads 'Not Guilty' and Turns the Charges Back on His Accusers and You." Steven Gaydos. *Los Angeles Reader,* December 11, 1992.

Producing, Financing and Distributing Film—A Comprehensive Legal and

Business Guide. 2d ed. Paul A. Baumgarten, Donald C. Farber, and Mark Fleischer. Limelight Editions, 1992.

"The Profit Participation Conundrum: A Glossary of Common Terms and Suggestions for Negotiation." Gunther H. Schiff. *Beverly Hills Bar Journal,* (Summer 1992).

"Profit Participation in the Motion Picture Industry." Steven D. Sills and Ivan L. Axelrod. *Los Angeles Lawyer,* April 1989.

"Profits the Thing, Not the Box Office Tally—Top-Grossing Pix Don't Always Bring Biggest Returns." Lawrence Cohn. *Variety,* October 5, 1992.

"Profits? What Profits?." D. Wechsler. *Forbes,* February 19, 1990.

"Projecting Profits from a Motion Picture" (excerpts from a self-published book). David J. Leedy. Lecture, UCLA Extension Class, "Contractual Aspects of Producing, Financing and Distributing Film," Fall 1991.

"Protecting Your Ideas in Hollywood." Lionel S. Sobel. *Writer's Friendly Legal Guide,* Writer's Digest Books, 1989.

Reel Power—The Struggle for Influence and Success in the New Hollywood. Mark Litwak. William Morrow, 1986.

Representation of Talent in a Feature Film. Entertainment Law Section. Beverly Hills Bar Association, 1992.

The Role of Production Counsel in Feature Films. Beverly Hills Bar Association, 1990.

"Rules of the Game—Between the Story Idea and the Movie Screen, There's a Long List of Executive No-No's." Jack Mathews. *American Film Magazine,* March 1990.

They Can Kill You But They Can't Eat You . . . and Other Lessons From the Front. Dawn Steel. Simon and Schuster's Pocket Books, 1993.

What a Producer Does. Buck Houghton. American Film Institute, 1991.

Who's Who in the Motion Picture Industry. Packard Publishing (updated periodically).

"Why Savvy Independents are 'Cocooning' with the Major Studios. Robert Marich. *The Hollywood Reporter Entertainment Financing Special Report,* p. S-8, January 1991.

Writer's Legal and Business Guide. Beverly Hills Bar Association. 1989.

You'll Never Eat Lunch in This Town Again. Julia Phillips. Penguin Books, 1991.

4

Independent-Distributor Financing

Independent distributors, by definition, are those film distributors who are not regularly or substantially affiliated with a so-called major studio/distributor. This diverse group includes such distributors as New Line Cinema, Samuel Goldwyn, Concorde, Castle Hill, First Run, IFEX, Shapiro Glickenhaus, Expanded Entertainment, Taurus Releasing, Fries Entertainment, Triton Pictures and Greycat. Until its recent purchase by Disney, Miramax was considered one of the leading independent distributors.

Most independent distributors tend to specialize in foreign distribution since the vast majority of the desirable theatre screens in the United States are taken up by major studio product. Many of the independent distributors thus are members of the American Film Marketing Association (AFMA), the film-industry trade group that represents the interests of non-major licensers of English language films in the international arena. The AFMA, located in Los Angeles, will be happy to provide inquiring producers with a current list of its member companies.

Some independent distributors do have production divisions, but they do not have the financial resources of the major studios and thus do not develop and produce as many in-house films as the majors, nor do they offer many P-F/D deals. Thus, generally speaking, an independent producer is less likely to be able to submit an undeveloped motion picture concept to an independent production company/distributor and obtain a development deal, although some low-budget projects would be more welcome at the independent's shop than at the studios.

The independent production/company distributors also have smaller amounts of money to commit to P-F/D arrangements and quite often require cofinancing deals. This, of course, means that the independent producer needs to provide at least half of the production money financing for a picture before the independent distributor will commit to putting up the other half of the production money along with funds to cover distribution expenses. Some of the independent distributors will subcontract with a major studio/distributor for a picture's domestic release.

A few of the independent distributors are considered credit-worthy enough in the eyes of entertainment lenders to support negative pickup or presale production financing arrangements (see chapters 11 and 13).

Most of the independent distributors are simply not capable of serving as sources of production financing and either acquire feature film product using a pure acquisition distribution agreement that then obligates that distributor to put up some or all of the money to cover distribution expenses or accept product on a rent-a-distributor basis, a distribution arrangement requiring that the independent producer not only finance the production of his or her film independent of the distributor but also put up some or all of the money to cover distribution expenses. In the rent-a-distributor situation, the distributor, of course, provides its services for a lower distribution fee and does not recoup any distribution costs since it usually does not incur any.

Advantages

Available for smaller films. Independent distributors may finance or participate in the financing of a feature film project that the major studios are not or would not be interested in, since in the view of the majors the film does not lend itself to a high enough budget or does not appeal to a broad cross section of the movie-going audience.

More personal attention. Independent distributors can often provide more specialized handling of independently produced feature films, if for no other reason than they have fewer films during the course of a year to divide their attention and resources.

Support for the film. Independent distributors are more likely to work closely with an independent producer in the release of a picture and to place a film in theatres that will allow a picture to "find" its audience by leaving a picture on the screen for a longer period of time.

Negotiating leverage. The negotiating leverage of an independent distributor is more closely aligned with that of an independent producer; thus, the independent producer is more likely to be able to negotiate a distribution agreement that is not unconscionable (i.e., heavily weighted in favor of the distributor).

Chances of net profits. Independent producers might reasonably assume that since the agreements negotiated with independent distributors are more likely to be fair than distribution agreements with major studio/distributors, the chances of a film distributed by an independent distributor achieving net profits may be greater than with a major studio/distributor.

Disadvantages

Limited financial resources. Independent distributors generally do not have the financial resources of a major studio/distributor and are thus less likely to provide development deals, full production financing on a P-F/D basis, or provide discountable distribution agreement/guarantees to support negative pickups or presales.

Bankruptcies. Each year a number of independent distributors go out of business, making it impossible for them to fulfill their financial obligations to the independent producers of films currently in distribution. It is difficult for independent producers to make an informed judgment about the financial stability of independent distributors (but see *Smaller pool of revenues* below).

Booking limitations. Independent distributors do not have as much leverage with domestic exhibitors and are thus generally less able to book films in the better theatres.

Less collections clout. Independent distributors generally do not have the collection capabilities of the major studio/distributors and are thus not as able to gain favorable treatment from exhibitors in the settlement transaction.

Smaller pool of revenues. Collectively, films distributed by independent U.S.-based distributors in the domestic theatrical marketplace on the average only garner about 7.5 percent of the box office gross each year; thus, the pool of distributor rentals for independently distributed films is significantly less than the pool of distributor rentals for films released by the majors.

Further Reading

The AIVF Guide to Film and Video Distributors. Edited by Kathryn Bowser. Association of Video/Filmmakers.

Distributing Independent Film and Videos. Morrie Warshawski. The Media Project (Portland, Oregon), FIVF-New York, 1989.

Entertainment Industry Economics. 2d ed. Harold L. Vogel. Cambridge University Press, 1990.

Film and Video Financing. Michael Wiese. Michael Wiese Productions, 1991.

Film Finance and Distribution—A Dictionary of Terms. John W. Cones. Silman-James Press, 1992

Film Industry Contracts. John W. Cones. Self-published, 1993.

"Financing the Production of Theatrical Motion Pictures." Lionel S. Sobel. *Entertainment Law Reporter,* May 1984.

Hollywood Distributors Directory. Published by Hollywood Creative Directory (annual publication).

How I Made a Hundred Movies in Hollywood and Never Lost a Dime. Roger Corman and Jim Jerome. Random House, 1990.

Independent Feature Film Production—A Complete Guide from Concept to Distribution. Gregory Goodell. St. Martin's Press, 1982.

Independent Film Markets. Paul Kagan Associates (published twice monthly).

"Legal Aspects of Film Financing." Barsky, Hertz, Ros, and Vinnik. (seminar handout), April 1990.

"Lessons In Self Defense—Distribution Contracts and Arbitration Clauses." Mark Litwak. *The Independent,* July 1993.

"Long-Term Contracts for Independent Producers." Nigel Sinclair. *Entertainment Law and Finance,* November 1986.

"Making Millions and Going Broke, How Production Companies Make Fortunes and Bankrupt Themselves." David Royal. *American Premiere,* November/December, 1991.

Making Money in Film and Video. 2d ed. Raul daSilva. Focal Press, 1992.

"Maximizing Producers' Negative Pick-Up Profits." John W. Cones. *Entertainment Law and Finance,* June 1992.

Motion Picture Marketing and Distribution. Fred Goldberg. Focal Press, 1991.

"Movie Industry Update—Investment Research." Richard P. Simon. Goldman Sachs (annual publication).

Movie Stats. Paul Kagan Associates (monthly newsletter).

The Next Step: Distributing Independent Films and Videos. Edited by Morrie Warshawski. Association of Independent Video/Filmmakers.

Producing, Financing and Distributing Film: A Comprehensive Legal and Business Guide. 2d ed. Paul A. Baumgarten, Donald C. Farber, and Mark Fleischer. Limelight Editions, 1992.

"Profit Participation in the Motion Picture Industry." Steven D. Sills and Ivan L. Axelrod. *Los Angeles Lawyer,* April 1989.

"Representing Independent Motion Picture Producers." Sinclair and Gerse. *Los Angeles Lawyer*, May 1988.

"Safe Harbor—In 1990s, Indies Quickly Discovering Best Lifeline Is Tied to a Major Distributor." Judy Brennan. *Daily Variety*, p. 12, June 26, 1991.

"Strategies for the International Production and Distribution of Feature Films in the 1990's." Thomas J. Cryan, David W. Johnson, James S. Crane, and Anthony Cammarata. *Loyola Entertainment Law Journal* 8, 1988.

5

Domestic Studio Facilities Deals

Often in discussions, books or articles relating to the film industry, the term *studio* is used to refer to the so-called major studio/distributor organizations of affiliated companies, most of which own a physical studio facility, one or more film production companies, one or more distribution companies, and in some cases even interests in theatre chains; that is, they are vertically integrated. On the other hand, not all of these so-called majors actually have the sound stages or studio lots that technically make it possible to accurately refer to the organization as a studio. Thus, the term *studio* can be a bit misleading at times. After all, there are a number of pure studios situated around the country that are not affiliated with production companies, have no distribution subsidiary and certainly own no interests in theatres. Those studios are the organizations that own and provide (for film production company use) the physical locations and other facilities including soundstages, sets, prop departments, offices, commissaries, and the like for development, preproduction, production and postproduction of feature films, as well as other film or video productions.

Some of the local studios were created without the benefit of a well-thought-out business plan. For example, most every state in the United States has a film commission—at the state, regional and/or local levels. Those film commissions generally do not get involved in film finance other than possibly helping to sponsor a seminar from time to time or encouraging the publication of a directory that may include film finance consultants, attorneys or other specialists who can provide useful information. The primary mission of the film commissions is generally seen as "bringing in production to the state or local community," that is, productions that already have funding. Unfortunately for those film commissions, there is a limited number of films that have financing and are available to be shot on location, and thus the film commission business has become extremely competitive. As a result, film commissioners have had well-meaning discussions with local businesspeople about what can be done in the state or community to attract more location shoots in their jurisdiction, and inevitably some of these business people come up with the bright idea of building a movie studio.

Regardless of whether the above-described scenario was instrumental in bringing them about, domestic studio production facilities now exist or are being created in California, North Carolina, Hawaii, Florida, Texas, Tennessee and other states all around the country. Again, unfortunately, for those studios, there simply does not appear to be enough business available for such studios to prosper—thus, the development of the domestic studio facility deal.

The domestic studio facility deal, much like the "foreign facility deal" discussed in chapter 38, involves an offer by a local studio to provide certain below-the-line goods and/or services for either below-market prices or for an ownership interest in the film. Such goods and/or services might include studio facilities (i.e., sound stages, actor suites and production offices), production equipment, local casting, catering services, some local crew persons, locations, below-cost housing arrangements, postproduction services and so forth.

The local studio (in cooperation with the local film commission) ultimately hopes to create a reputation for the local community as a good place to shoot feature films and thus eventually to create jobs and help the local economy by bringing in money that will be spent there. Unfortunately for the local studios, many feature films can be shot in a variety of locales; thus, the enterprising independent producers merely keep shopping around for the best deal available on below-the-line goods and services offered by the domestic studio facilities. Thus, the domestic studio facility does not ever seem to become a viable business that can offer its facilities at more profitable rates.

Advantages

Production cost savings.   The producer is able to shoot a film and expend less money on below-the-line budget items.

From the studio's point of view.   The studio hopes that the production brought in on a facilities deal basis will create positive word of mouth for the studio in the production community and other productions will follow (hopefully at regular rates).

Disadvantages

Savings versus quality. The pressure on the producer to save money in the production of the film may have detrimental effects on the quality of the motion picture; that is, the equipment, locations, facilities and the like gained in the domestic studio deal may not be up to par.

Savings not offset. The savings gained in the domestic studio deal may not offset the cost of transporting and housing the cast and crew that are brought in from other locations such as Los Angeles.

Further Reading

Feature Films on a Low Budget. John Randall. Focal Press, 1991.

Film Finance and Distribution—A Dictionary of Terms. John W. Cones. Silman-James Press, 1992.

Making Money in Film and Video. 2d ed. Raul daSilva. Focal Press, 1992.

Motion Picture Marketing and Distribution. Fred Goldberg. Focal Press, 1991.

"Producer Looks to Lure Film/TV to Nashville Stages." Clark Parsons. *Daily Variety*, p. 8, August 9, 1993.

Producing, Financing and Distributing Film: A Comprehensive Legal and Business Guide. 2d ed. Paul A. Baumgarten, Donald C. Farber, and Mark Fleischer. Limelight Editions, 1992.

"State-Funded Studio Underway in Hawaii." Jerry Hopkins. *Variety*, p. 33, February 24, 1992.

6

Film Laboratory Deals

In the rush to compete for film-processing business, some of the smaller film labs have come up with creative ways to bring in new accounts. As an example, one specific film lab in California has recently offered the following deal:

- The lab agrees to provide goods and services valued up to $400,000 on a deferred basis
- The lab will participate in the film's net profits
- The lab's net profit participation may range from 25 to 34 percent depending on the value of the goods and services provided
- The proceeds from sales or distribution will be used to first pay back the lab's investment, then afterwards that of the other investors and producers (i.e., the lab has to be in a first position to recoup the value of its goods and services)
- After all expenses of production and all investments have been paid, the remaining distributor gross receipts are considered net profits and are divided as received in accordance with the respective percentage shares
- The lab must be in a *para-passu* (equal and concurrent) ownership position with respect to all cash investors
- The producer is obligated to use the distribution services of an independent feature film distribution company that is affiliated with the lab
- The distributor has approval rights over the film's final budget and script

The lab's goods and services may include: negative raw stock, negative developing, dailies, sound transfers, editorial cutting rooms, film projection, film coding, opticals, titles, sound editorial, negative cutting, ADR and Foley, sound re-recording, optical transfers, color dupe, inter-positive, inter-negative, first trial answer print, release prints and film to video transfer.

This particular lab also offers certain film completion services through an affiliated company, and if the producer can demonstrate good credit, the lab may be able to arrange a camera, sound, lighting

30

and grip package together with electronic editing on a deferred financed basis.

Knowing that some labs offer such deals, producers looking to finance the production of a feature film may want to inquire of a number of labs to determine whether they offer similar arrangements. It would not be difficult for a film lab to establish relationships with film production equipment houses and independent distributors, although the terms of such package deals may vary widely.

Advantages

Lower production costs. Obtaining lab goods and services on a deferred basis lowers the producer's (or investors') out-of-pocket production and postproduction costs.

One-stop shopping. Depending on the particular lab, a number of related services may be arranged for all at once, for example, lab services, production equipment rental and distribution.

Disadvantages

Likelihood of net profits. If the lab's affiliated distributor is no better than other distributors in functioning as the film's collecting and disbursing agent, the producers and other investors, if any, are not likely to see any net profits.

Quality of lab work. Since the lab is offering its services on a deferred basis, this might suggest that there is some question about the ability of the lab to provide quality services.

Further Reading

Feature Films on a Low Budget. John Randall. Focal Press, 1991.
Film Finance and Distribution—A Dictionary of Terms. John W. Cones. Silman-James Press, 1992.
Film Industry Contracts. John W. Cones. Self-published, 1993.
Making Money in Film and Video. 2d ed. Raul daSilva. Focal Press, 1992.
Motion Picture Marketing and Distribution. Fred Goldberg. Focal Press, 1991.

7

Talent Agency Financing

Talent agencies have traditionally limited their activities to finding employment for actors, directors, writers and sometimes producers. However, some of the more powerful agencies in recent years have begun to realize that they could substantially increase their fees by attaching two or more of their own clients to the same film project and at the same time increase the chances of the film's being made since a studio might be reluctant to pass on an attractive package offered by such an agency. It was only a matter of time, then, that these same aggressive talent agencies realized that they could take their involvement in film packaging to still another level by also arranging for the financing of their packaged film projects outside the studios.

To accomplish this end, some of the talent agencies brought in or developed in-house expertise in film finance. Although, not truly a stand-alone form of film finance, it is important for independent producers to recognize that some talent agencies can help assemble financing for a package with which a number of their clients are involved. The talent agencies are not putting up their own money to finance the production costs of feature films; they are merely becoming involved in putting together the financing arrangements and going beyond the traditional studio sources of financing by considering below-the-line facilities deals, international coproductions, foreign government subsidies, presales and so forth (see discussions of those forms of finance in later chapters).

Advantages

One-stop shopping. It is now possible for the producer of a film project to approach a top talent agency (assuming the project is of interest to the agency) not only to get help attaching one actor to the film but possibly attaching a director and several actors, while also arranging for production financing and distribution through the agency's industry relationships.

From the agency's point of view. Combining talent and financing packaging significantly increases the agency's opportunities to be compensated. Not only can the agency extract its usual 10 percent commission (for each of its clients in the package) under such circumstances, but it may be able to build in an executive producing fee for the agency in addition to or in lieu of the commission.

Disadvantages

Multiple conflicts of interest. Not only is there a built-in conflict of interest in a situation where an agency tries to attach two of its clients to the same project, but such conflicts multiply when more of the agency's clients are attached to a project and the agency also arranges for financing. Consequently, the agency's interests tend to prevail in such situations and the interests of others (financial or creative), including actors, writers, producers and in some cases financiers, are subordinated.

Producer conflict. Talent agency involvement in packaging and film finance means the agents have moved into an activity traditionally undertaken by producers.

Further Reading

Antitrust Compliance Manual: A Guide for Counsel, Management, and Public Officials. Walker B. Comebys. Practicing Law Institute, 1986.

Competitive Business Practices. 2d ed. Allan Browne. The State Bar of California and the University of California, 1991.

Film Finance and Distribution—A Dictionary of Terms. John W. Cones. Silman-James Press, 1992.

Film Industry Contracts. John W. Cones. Self-published, 1993.

Film Producers, Studios, Agents and Casting Directors (directory). Lone Eagle Publishing (updated periodically).

Motion Picture Marketing and Distribution. Fred Goldberg. Focal Press, 1991.

"Pic Banker Afman Joins ICM to Run New Finance Unit." Andrea King. *The Hollywood Reporter,* July 12, 1991.

Producing, Financing and Distributing Film: A Comprehensive Legal and Business Guide. 2d ed. Paul A. Baumgarten, Donald C. Farber, and Mark Fleischer. Limelight Editions, 1992.

Representation of Talent in a Feature Film. Entertainment Law Section. Beverly Hills Bar Association, 1992.

"Talent for the Game." Robert Marich. *The Hollywood Reporter Finance Special Report*, 1993.

What a Producer Does. Buck Houghton. American Film Institute, 1991.

Who's Who in the Motion Picture Industry. Packard Publishing (updated periodically).

8

End-User Financing

Presales could conceivably be considered a form of end-user financing. However, end-user financing is more generally associated with a cash investment by the end user put up in exchange for an equity percentage participation in the film's revenues in specified territories and/or media. In a presale the end user is not actually putting up any money to be used in producing the movie but instead is putting up a guarantee to pay a specified sum of money upon delivery of the film, and the actual production money (in a presale) comes from a lender.

Ancillary end users. Entities that exploit films in the ancillary markets, for example, video or cable companies, may prove useful sources of end-user financing. Ancillary markets are those geographical or technological areas of demand for film product that are auxiliary or supplemental to the theatrical market. The ancillary markets include foreign, network and syndicated television, pay cable and home video.

End users in the foreign marketplace. Foreign entities, such as television networks, entertainment consortiums, foreign conglomerates or foreign theatrical and home video distributors, who purchase rights to exploit U.S.-made films in foreign markets provide another possible source for end-user financing. Some of those entities are capable of financing a domestic film production and/or distribution company and may do so in exchange for product flow in their base territory and some level of participation in worldwide revenues (or the revenues of specific territories or dividends of the company).

Advantages

In best position. End users in the marketplace, whether foreign, domestic, theatrical, video or cable, are the business entities that are in the best position to make money from a producer's movie since, at the very least, they exercise the most control over that portion of the motion picture's revenue stream generated in their home territory. Therefore, they should be more willing than most to contribute toward the financing of the production costs of a given film. It then becomes a question of (a) identifying the end users, (b) how much to pay for specified rights and (c) what form the investment takes.

Knowing the audience. With end-user financing, the producer's financing partner is an industry entity that has expertise at the retail level, that is, its representatives are on the front lines when it comes to making judgments about the tastes of the movie-going public. Thus, it may be safe to presume that such a financing partner will not invest money in projects that it does not believe have commercial appeal in its market.

Disadvantages

Piecemeal financing. This form of financing typically is piecemeal in nature. It generally will require obtaining commitments from many end users (or some end users plus other financing sources) to cover the costs associated with producing the picture.

For producers with a track record. Generally speaking, only producers with track records, that is, producers who have successfully brought recognizable or commercially successful films in on time and under budget, will be able to attract foreign or domestic end-user financing.

Further Reading

"Banks, Investors Still Shy on Indies." Linda Keslar. *Variety*, November 16, 1992.

Feature Films on a Low Budget. John Randall. Focal Press, 1991.

Film Finance and Distribution—A Dictionary of Terms. John W. Cones. Silman-James Press, 1992.

Film Industry Contracts. John W. Cones. Self-published, 1993.

Making Money in Film and Video. 2d ed. Raul daSilva. Focal Press, 1992.

Role of Production Counsel in Feature Films. Beverly Hills Bar Association Education Publications.

"Strategies for the International Production and Distribution of Feature Films in the 1990's." Thomas J. Cryan, David W. Johnson, James S. Crane and Anthony Cammarata. *Loyola Entertainment Law Journal* 8 (1988).

9

Completion Funds

Feature film completion funds crop up from time to time. Examples include Cinema America, a $15 million film and video financing entity based in Houston, and the New York Completion Fund based in Cold Spring, New York. Film Dallas also functioned as a completion fund for some of the films in which it invested in the late eighties.

Completion funds are designed to provide partial production or postproduction financing. Such funds may be provided for films that have almost completed principal photography, for films that are complete except for postproduction or for films that are complete through postproduction but cannot be taken out of the lab because lab fees have not been paid.

The completion fund managers understandably assert that it is easier to make judgments regarding the prospects of a film when it is nearly complete than at the script stage. Thus, they feel it is safer to invest in nearly completed films as opposed to investing earlier. An additional part of the completion fund strategy is to spread the risk; that is, such funds seldom put up all of the money required to produce a film. Thus, they are sharing the downside risk with other investors and/or financiers. Furthermore, these providers of the final dollars are usually successful in negotiating a higher-per-dollar percentage interest in the film than earlier investors because without the last money in, the early money has no chance of recouping.

Another related type of fund, not otherwise covered in this book, is the so-called P&A (prints and ads) fund. For example, private interests and the state of Florida have recently created the Florida Film and Television Investment Trust Fund that, when operational, will apparently have the authority to invest up to $3 million to be used for prints and advertising on any completed film that spends 40 percent or more of its production budget in the state of Florida.

Advantages

Financing source of last resort. Producers generally approach film completion funds because they have run out of money on a film project that is nearly complete. Thus, the producer is in a bind, and the completion fund may represent the only possibility for salvaging the film project.

Investment versus loan. Many completion funds will invest in film projects and thus share in the risk as opposed to merely lending money in which case there is an obligation for the producer to repay such loans at a specific time.

Disadvantages

Weak bargaining position. Precisely because the producer is having problems, the completion fund entity is generally in a stronger bargaining position and thus can extract more favorable terms from the producer than earlier investors. This means that the producer and possibly the earlier investors and/or financiers may have to reduce their financial interests in the backside of the picture relative to the completion fund.

Limited funds. Generally speaking, completion funds will not invest large amounts of money per film.

Further Reading

"Cinema America Creates Film Fund." *The Hollywood Reporter*, p. 85, December 14, 1990.

"Completion Cache." *The Independent*, 9, November 1991.

Feature Films on a Low Budget. John Randall. Focal Press, 1991.

Film Finance and Distribution—A Dictionary of Terms. John W. Cones. Silman-James Press, 1992.

Film Industry Contracts. John W. Cones. Self-published, 1993.

"Florida Semi-Privatizes Location Promo—Agency May Become Financial Partner in Fla.-Made Pix." Jack Zink. *Variety*, April 19, 1993.

Motion Picture Marketing and Distribution. Fred Goldberg. Focal Press, 1991.

"Safe Haven." Birgit Heidsiek. *Off-Hollywood Report*, p. 16, Winter 1992.

PART 2

Lender Financing

10

Lender Financing Without Distributor Contracts

Loans may be used to finance the development, production and/or distribution expenses associated with a feature film. The loans discussed in this section are those not involving a preproduction distribution agreement and guarantee provided to the film's producer who then takes the agreement/guarantee to a bank or other lender that actually lends the funds, using the distributor's commitment as the effective collateral for the loan (see chapters 11 and 13). Instead, this section focuses on loans that may be provided by banks or other lenders, including individuals, that either require collateral in the form of hard assets or are willing to provide unsecured loans.

A loan is defined as the delivery of a sum of money to another under contract to return an equivalent amount at some future time with or without an additional sum agreed upon for its use. The characterization of a transaction as a loan or some other type of borrowing has significance in ascertaining whether usury laws apply to the amount of interest being charged and whether the securities laws apply to the transaction. The securities laws generally do not apply to loans.

Independent producers whose films are being financed by a studio or others who charge interest on the production monies provided may want to consider whether usury laws apply to the transaction. Usury is an unconscionable or exorbitant rate of interest, that is, an excessive and illegal requirement of compensation for forbearance on a debt (interest). State legislatures in each state determine the maximum allowable rates of interest that may be demanded in any financial transaction. However, usury laws generally do not apply to corporate borrowers. In all likelihood, the usury laws will not apply to studio loans since the studio will require that the production company be incorporated. On the other hand, it would be interesting and revealing to know if the interest rates charged by the major studio/distributors would be considered usurious if the loans had been made to individuals, since if the only difference between an individual borrower and a corporate borrower is some paperwork, it would appear that the corporate vehicle is merely being inserted into the transaction to circumvent the usury laws.

To obtain a bank loan, it is almost always necessary to offer some collateral, that is, to place within the legal control of the lender some property that may be sold in the event of a default and applied to the amount owed. Collateral is an asset pledged to a lender until a loan is repaid, that is, property, including accounts, contract rights, and chattel paper that have been sold, that is subject to a security interest.

Third party (nonbank) feature film development loans (a) may be secured by some form of hard asset and (b) are usually recourse to the borrower, that is, the lender can seek repayment directly from the borrower personally in the event of default. (Again, banks are not likely to make loans for significant amounts of funds unless such loans are collateralized with assets.) If a corporate production company is the borrower, the lender may also make the principals of the corporation personally liable for repayment of the loan. In addition, other guarantors may be required to assure repayment of the loan's principal and interest.

Recourse loans. Often loans to film producers will be made on a recourse basis; that is, the loan will be made only if an endorser or guarantor (e.g., the producer) is made personally liable for payment in the event the borrower (e.g., the production company) defaults.

Debt or equity transaction. Both the lender and the borrowing producer should be careful to insure that what is intended as a loan to be used for development of a screenplay or preproduction expenses can be fairly characterized as debt and is not characterized as an equity investment, if in fact debt is what is desired. If the transaction is characterized as some form of equity participation, (a) the lender actually becomes an investor whose investment is at risk and thus (b) there may be no obligation for the producer to repay the loan (which on the surface sounds good for the producer), but characterization as an equity investment may also result in (a) the producer's having sold an unregistered security to a passive investor, thus triggering securities compliance requirements, and (b) the creation of an entity (e.g., joint venture or association) that may have to bear unfavorable tax consequences.

The factors that determine whether a transaction creates debt or equity include the following:

Recourse—whether the loan is a nonrecourse loan or a recourse loan (a nonrecourse loan secured only by the film is more likely than a recourse loan to be considered an equity investment)

Fixed repayment date—whether a fixed repayment date has been established (a fixed repayment date suggests that the transaction should be characterized as a loan)

Secured loan—whether the transaction is secured (security suggests a loan)

Interest tied to profits—whether the rate of interest on the "loan" is tied to the amount of profits earned by the film (if the interest rate increases with the level of profits, that increases the chances that the transaction would be characterized as an equity investment)

Creative control—whether the lender exercises substantial control over the production (the more control exercised, the less likely the transaction would be characterized as a loan)

Subordination—whether the "lender" subordinates, that is, takes a second position to third parties with respect to payments made from the film's revenues (subordination suggests something other than a loan)

Other lenders—whether another lender would have lent funds on the same or similar basis.

Imputed interest. If the lender on a film actually provides the producer with a below-market interest rate, the Internal Revenue Service (IRS), based on Code Section 7872, may, in certain circumstances, add interest to the transaction. This only rarely occurs and such rules would only be involved if the relationship between the producer/borrower and the lender indicates that the lower interest rate was intended to transfer wealth from the lender to the producer/borrower, as is sometimes the case in father-son transactions.

Advantages

Lender does not share in net profits. Producers who borrow money from a lender are generally not obligated to allow the lender to share in any of the film's net profits or net proceeds (or the producer's share of such moneys); that is, the lender's consideration for making the loan is generally limited to the interest charged.

No lender creative control. Lenders do not generally exercise any creative control over the production of a motion picture.

Noncollateralized loans. Loans not supported by collateral may be suitable for development money or the financing of an ultralow budget picture.

Disadvantages

Must be repaid. Loans generally have to be repaid regardless of whether the film makes money.

Incorporation requirement. Most lenders will require that the production company organize as a corporation so as to avoid any possibility of usury problems. Incorporating adds additional expense to the transaction for the producer and creates an entity that must be properly maintained by the producer over the years.

Collateral may be lost. A feature film production money loan supported by hard asset collateral, for example, the family ranch, is a good way to lose the ranch.

Noncollateralized loans are limited. Loans not supported by collateral are generally not available except for small amounts of money.

Specific term. Loans are generally repayable at a specified time, regardless of whether any of the revenues generated by the motion picture in any markets and media have been received by the borrower/producer.

Completion guarantor required. A sophisticated lender may require that the producer contract with a completion guarantor to protect the lender against the risk of budget overruns, thus causing the producer to expend moneys on the completion guarantor's fees and in all likelihood causing the production budget to be otherwise increased so as to decrease the chances of exceeding the budget.

Personal liability may be required. Some lenders may make the producer personally liable for the repayment of the loan in addition to the liability of the corporate production company.

Tax consequences. Tax problems may occur if the lender provides the loan at below-market interest rates.

Further Reading

The Emerging Business: Managing for Growth. Seymour Jones and M. Bruce Cohen. Ronald Press, 1983.

Entertainment Industry Contracts—Motion Pictures. Vol. 1. Donald C. Farber. Matthew Bender, 1991.

Feature Films on a Low Budget. John Randall. Focal Press, 1991.

Film Finance and Distribution—A Dictionary of Terms. John W. Cones. Silman-James Press, 1992.

Film Industry Contracts. John W. Cones. Self-published, 1993.

Financing Your Film—A Guide for Independent Filmmakers and Producers. Trisha Curran. Praeger Publishers, 1986.

Law Dictionary. 2d ed. Steven H. Gifis. Barron's Educational Series, 1984.

11

Negative Pickups

The term *negative pickup* usually refers to the commitment made by a distributor to a producer to purchase or license feature film distribution rights from the producer and the distributor's guarantee to pay an agreed-upon purchase price (pickup price) when the distributor picks up the negative after delivery of the completed picture. The commitment is usually made prior to the start of production and certainly prior to the completion of the film. If the negative pickup deal is with a distributor that meets the criteria of entertainment lenders—for example, a major studio, and sometimes a financially stable independent distributor—the producer may be able to take the distribution agreement and guarantee to such a bank or lender where it can be discounted, that is, for a fee paid to the bank, converted into an amount of cash less than the face value of the contract. Such funds may then be used to pay for some or all of the production costs of the film. Sometimes, the term *negative pickup* or *pickup* is used to refer to a sale or license of distribution rights at any time, even after completion of the film. However, when a film is independently financed and presented to a distributor for pickup, that transaction is more accurately referred to as an *acquisition* or *pure acquisition*, which is documented by an acquisition/distribution agreement. At least it would be less confusing if the term *negative pickup* was reserved for use with the lender-financed transaction described above, the term *acquisition* was reserved for use with the independently financed transaction and the term *pickup* was dropped from the film industry vocabulary altogether.

Some speculative numbers. As an example, Universal recently has indicated it acquires 6 to 7 films each year by virtue of the negative pickup deal (3 others are purely in-house productions; 12 to 13 more are P-F/D deals). Hypothetically speaking, if the other 7 majors also picked up 7 films a year, that would mean the majors would be acquiring approximately 56 films a year by means of the negative pickup (or the pure acquisition deal). If the other 7 majors utilize the production-financing/distribution arrangement to finance, let's say 10 films each, that's another 80 films. If each then also produces 3 films apiece as purely in-house product, that's another 24 films. That would account for approximately 160 films, which is pretty close to what the majors distribute each year (if not slightly higher).

A method of financing. Traditionally, the term *negative pickup* has referred to the sale or grant of film distribution rights made prior to completion of the picture and as a means of obtaining production financing. When the negative pickup is used as a method of financing a motion picture, the producer sells or licenses the film to a distributor in exchange for the distributor's promise to pay the agreed-upon purchase price (pickup price), when the distributor *picks up the negative* after delivery of the completed picture. The producer may then take the negative pickup distributor commitment to a commercial bank, use the pickup letter as collateral, and borrow production funds from the bank, which discounts the agreement, that is, converts the distributor commitment (paper) into an amount of cash less than the face value of the distributor's commitment. A distributor's pickup commitment letter or agreement can also sometimes be used to facilitate the raising of production funds from investors since the pickup letter documents strong distributor interest in the project and presumably provides the investors with an improved chance to recoup at least a portion of their investment (assuming the distributor has the financial wherewithal to support its commitment).

Negative pickup deal variables. The important variables in such transactions include whether an advance payment is made to the producer upon signing of the negative pickup distribution agreement (and if so, how much), whether an advance is paid to the producer upon delivery of the completed film (and if so, how much), whether the distributor provides a guarantee to the producer and whether the producer obtains a continuing participation in the revenue stream generated by the exploitation of the motion picture.

Producer considerations. In addition to the financial stability of the distributor, a principal consideration for the producer is the pickup price. Usually the price will be pegged to the estimated negative cost of the picture. The amount of the producer's profit participation, if any, will vary depending on a number of factors, such as the amount committed to be paid by the distributor, the rights acquired, the anticipated prospects for the picture and the perceived risk for the distributor.

47

Typical provisions. The negative pickup distribution agreement is typically a lengthy contract. The principal variable provisions include the rights granted, the territory, the term of distribution, the consideration (pickup price) and the producer's percentage participation in net profits (or net proceeds).

Producer negotiating strategy. In negotiating the negative pickup distribution agreement, the producer should try to avoid or minimize contingencies to the distributor's performance. The producer should eliminate as many grounds as possible that the distributor may be able to use as a basis for refusing delivery of the film: for example, the final picture reflects insignificant differences from the approved script or even more subjective grounds for refusing the completed picture.

What the distributor wants. In negotiating the negative pickup distribution agreement, the distributor will typically ask for all rights of every kind in all territories. The distributor will take the position that it is entitled to all rights since its domestic theatrical advertising and promotional expenditures for the film will enhance the value of all other rights. The distributor also will want to be able to use its sole discretion relating to the manner, method and timing of distribution of the motion picture and in the exploitation of the picture's ancillary rights.

Drafting the agreement. One of the major problems involved in drafting a negative pickup distribution agreement is describing in words the motion picture that the producer is obligated to deliver. The script must be mutually agreed upon and adhered to during production, unless provisions are included for distributor approval of necessary changes. Otherwise, deviations from the script during production may render the film unacceptable to the distributor. The negative pickup/distribution agreement must include references to and guarantee the involvement of certain key people in the production of the film, such as the director and principal cast members. The agreement must also define acceptable standards of technical quality for the film. Disputes relating to this issue may be resolved by the film laboratory, although if the distributor picked the lab, there may be some question as to its loyalties. The distributor will also generally want the agreement to include a copy of the film's budget (as an exhibit) in order to provide assurances that the producer will have enough money to produce the type of motion picture anticipated by the distributor.

Contingency plans. Many things can go wrong in the production of a motion picture and often do. Thus, the producer should try to include contingency options in the agreement to provide for some producer flexibility in resolving problems that do occur, for example, script changes or actor replacements.

Retained rights. In some situations, the distributor acquires something less than all rights, with the producer retaining specified territorial or media rights that he or she has already presold or intends to exploit through separate agreements with third parties. The producer's ability to retain such rights depends first on the willingness of the producer to ask for such concessions and then on the relative bargaining strength of the parties. Unfortunately, few producers have the kind of leverage required to extract such concessions from distributors.

Clearance. The producer must ensure that he or she has or will obtain by the time of conveyance to the distributor all rights that he or she intends to transfer. The producer must secure the copyright in the underlying property and must procure any necessary release from persons who may have claims relating to the subject matter of the motion picture. The producer must also ensure that he or she has complied or will be able to comply with all of the distributor's delivery requirements such as lists of credits and insurance certificates.

Delivery requirements. The producer or the producer's attorney must be very careful in examining the distributor's description of delivery requirements for the film, as well as the required production elements such as cast, director, script and budget. If the distributor can refuse delivery on subjective grounds, the negative pickup agreement may not be acceptable to a financier. The producer will therefore try to eliminate from the negative pickup agreement with the distributor subjective grounds for refusing delivery, such as artistic quality, and try to focus the agreement on objective grounds such as technical quality.

Negative pickup versus distributor guarantee. The main difference between a negative pickup and a distributor guarantee is that the negative pickup does not necessarily imply that the distributor guarantees the repayment of any production loan or investor funds. Instead, the distributor merely agrees to distribute a producer's film contingent upon delivery of the completed picture pursuant to the terms of the delivery schedule. Sometimes the distributor will agree to pay the producer an advance against the film's profits, payable on delivery of the completed motion picture. Any overbudget costs in a negative pickup deal are solely the responsibility of the producer who must arrange for a completion bond that will guarantee delivery of a finished film. Thus, there is little or no risk for the distributor if for any reason the film is not finished or if the finished film in any way fails to meet the requirements set forth in the negative pickup agreement; that is, if the producer fails to deliver a completed film, the completion guarantor (among other options) may be obligated to repay the bank's loan.

Laboratory letter. Upon completion of the film, assuming that all the terms of the negative pickup distribution agreement have been met by the producer, the film lab (or other mutually agreed-upon third party) will issue a letter stating, among other things, that the finished film is of acceptable commercial quality, that the script adhered to the standards set out in the agreement and that the pre-approved cast members appear in the finished film in their proper roles. Upon receipt of the film and the laboratory letter, the distribution advance, if any, will be released to the producer (or to the lending institution to pay back the production loan).

The producer advance is recoupable. Sometimes, an advance payment is made with the balance paid upon delivery of the picture. It is not unusual for a payment made on signing and/or upon pickup to be considered an advance that is recoupable by the distributor out of the distributor's gross receipts or the producer's percentage participation in the net profits of the film. In some cases, the distributor will put the agreed-upon sum (advance) into an escrow account for payment to the producer on delivery of the motion picture. To the extent that the producer is able to negotiate a larger advance, the producer's percentage participation in the picture's net profits is likely to be reduced.

Security for production loan/comfort for investors. The producer may be able to use the negative pickup commitment as security for financial arrangements to fund production of the picture. For example, the producer may try to use the negative pickup agreement as security for a bank loan to provide production financing. The bank would then be paid all or most of its loan when the distributor pays its advance upon delivery of the picture. In the alternative, the producer may use the distributor commitment to provide assurances to an investor group (e.g., limited partnership) that distribution for the film is in place and, if a distributor guarantee is included, to reduce the downside risk for such investors.

Requirements of the distributor. The distributor will typically require that the completed picture meet certain requirements: (1) the film is in substantial compliance with the approved script, (2) specified cast members appear in their proper roles, (3) the approved director has directed the film, (4) the ceiling on the film's running time is adhered to, and (5) the film has a certain MPAA rating.

Producer participation in net profits. The question as to whether the producer will be able to participate in the picture's net profits will to some extent depend on the size of the advance negotiated by the producer, whether any portion of the advance was payable upon signing the negative pickup distribution agreement, and whether a distributor guarantee was provided.

Objective criteria for delivery. The negative pickup agreement should be self-executing; that is, if the producer completes the motion picture to the distributor's objective specifications, as set out in the negative pickup agreement, then the distributor is obligated to pay the specified sum and pick up the negative.

Distribution agreements are substantially similar. The terms and provisions found in a negative pickup distribution agreement are very much like those found in the P-F/D agreement and the acquisition/distribution agreement. The major differences relate to who provides production financing for the film and when the agreement is signed.

Advantages

Risk of no distribution. By producing a film without a distributor commitment, the producer assumes the risk that an acquisition/distribution deal may be difficult or even impossible to negotiate for the completed film. Thus, some producers regard a sale after completion of the motion picture as a less desirable method of proceeding than a prior distribution commitment. These producers sometimes prefer to make their distribution arrangements as early as possible, for example, as in the negative pickup arrangement. In other words, some production companies often prefer to resolve their distribution arrangements as early as possible because distribution may be difficult or even impossible to find. By not obtaining a negative pickup, the producer runs the risk that the film will not be as good as anticipated and that little or no distributor interest will develop after completion.

May be only alternative. If a studio development deal or a P-

F/D arrangement is not available to a given producer for a specific feature film and the producer is not inclined to go the investor-financing route, then the negative pickup arrangement may be the only available choice for financing a film.

The studio's perspective. From the studio's point of view, the studio/distributor is not taking a production risk in the negative pickup transaction because if the negative is not delivered, the studio/distributor has no obligation. This sometimes makes it easier for a producer to obtain a negative pickup deal with a studio than a production-financing/distribution agreement.

Obligation to pay. If the negative is delivered in accordance with the delivery requirements imposed by the studio/distributor in the negative pickup distribution agreement, but the picture is not very good in creative terms, the studio is still obligated to pay the pickup price.

Easier to get. Again, from the studio's perspective, one advantage of the negative pickup arrangement is that the distributor obtains a completed picture containing certain agreed-upon elements for a fixed sum of money, most if not all of which is payable only upon delivery of the picture. This again may make it easier for a producer to obtain a negative pickup commitment from a studio/distributor than a production-financing/distribution agreement.

Over budget risk. In the negative pickup arrangement, the distributor does not share in the risk that the film will go over budget, since a completion guarantee will have been provided by the producer. Any advance upon signing is usually so nominal (if any is provided at all) that the distributor runs very little financial risk if the film is not delivered as and when promised.

Competing distributors. Some distributors miss out on obtaining rights to a good picture because another competing distributor committed to distribution at an earlier stage. Thus, a producer may be able to use this possible occurrence to his or her advantage in extracting a negative pickup commitment from a distributor who fears that a competing distributor is going to obtain the rights to distribute what may well turn out to be a good movie.

Domestic distribution commitment. The negative pickup provides some assurance that the film will be distributed domestically. This may be an important factor in securing foreign or ancillary pre-sales.

Risk reduction. From the point of view of a lender or investors, the negative pickup removes most of the risk relating to lack of distribution in financing a motion picture.

Disadvantages

Production funding. The producer has to obtain production financing for the film from sources other than the studio or distributor.

More favorable terms. Some producers prefer to arrange production financing for a film without a distributor commitment, believing that if the picture turns out to be a very good film (as the producer envisions), the producer will be in a better position to negotiate more favorable terms in an acquisition/distribution agreement than in a negative pickup agreement.

Risk/reward ratio. As a general rule, the more risk the producer assumes relative to the distributor, the better the deal the producer will be able to negotiate. Thus, there is an incentive for a producer not to enter into a negative pickup agreement if the producer can secure financing without one.

Less expensive for distributor. Assuming the same level of quality for a movie, it is generally less expensive for a distributor to make the commitment to purchase a motion picture before the film is completed as opposed to after the film is completed. With a good movie in the can, a producer may try to create a bidding war between distributors for the right to distribute the film.

Speculative deal. From the distributor's perspective, the negative pickup can be highly speculative. No one can accurately predict the quality of a given film in its completed form as a motion picture.

Complex transactions. Negative pickups are complex, document intensive, time-consuming and difficult to get. For a producer without a substantially packaged property, a negative pickup deal and distributor guarantee are virtually impossible to obtain, and without both of them, a bank loan for production financing is usually out of the question.

A circuitous route. The negative pickup distribution deal and documentation can be complicated, particularly since the producer will be trying to take the negative pickup distribution agreement and guarantee, if any, to a lending source to get it to lend production funds before the picture is made. In that scenario, the producer will have to satisfy the requirements of the distributor in order to get the negative pickup distribution agreement (and possibly a guarantee), will have to get that agreement with a distributor (and on terms) that the lender approves, will have to obtain a completion bond for the picture from a completion guarantor that the lender approves and may have to provide additional collateral for the production loan, for example, presales or hard assets.

Those with a track record. Negative pickups usually go to feature film producers who have an established track record and relationships with studios, distributors, completion guarantors and lenders.

The lender's expertise. Negative pickup loans are generally only available through banks or other lenders based in Los Angeles or New York since they are typically the only lenders who have the expertise to make the required judgment regarding the creditworthiness of the distributor whose paper is being discounted.

Further Reading

"Banking on Success: 'That's Where the Money Is.' " *The Hollywood Reporter* (Entertainment Finance Special Report), August 1990.

"Banks, Investors Still Shy on Indies." Linda Keslar. *Variety*, November 16, 1992.

"CBC RIP: Independents Lose Their Biggest Backer." Paul Noglows. *Daily Variety*, June 1, 1992.

"Chemical's Equation: $285 Mil in Indie Loans." Robert Marich. *The Hollywood Reporter*, March 5, 1992.

"Entertainment Lending Institutions." *The Hollywood Reporter* (Independent Producers and Distributors Special Report), August 1991.

"Feature Film Secured Financing: A Transactional Approach for Lender's Counsel." Robert G. Weiss and Alan G. Benjamin. *Comm./Ent. L.J.* 5, no. 1 (1982).

Film and Video Financing. Michael Wiese. Michael Wiese Productions, 1991.

Film Finance and Distribution. John W. Cones. Silman-James Press, 1992.

Film Industry Contracts. John W. Cones. Self-published, 1993.

"Financing the Production of Theatrical Motion Pictures." Lionel S. Sobel. *Entertainment Law Reporter*, May 1984.

Financing Your Film—A Guide for Independent Filmmakers and Producers. Trisha Curran. Praeger Publishers, 1986.

"Hollywood's Family Ways—Who Can You Trust Better Than Kin?" Terry Pristin. *Los Angeles Times*, January 31, 1993.

"Independent Feature Film Discountable-Contract Finance: A Transactional Guide to Negative-Pickup and Presale Financing Arrangements." Jeffrey C. Foy. Self-published, 1993.

Independent Feature Film Production—A Complete Guide from Concept to Distribution. Gregory Goodell. St. Martin's Press, 1982.

"Indie Financing Problems Set as Opening Discussion for Santa Monica Confab." Hy Hollinger. *Variety*, February 24, 1992.

"Is the Bond Biz Coming Unglued?" Paul Noglows. *Variety*, April 12, 1993.

"Majors Are Relying on Indies in a Major Way—Number of Outside Pix on Studios' Slates Is Rising." Lawrence Cohn. *Variety*, April 27, 1992.

"Maximizing Producers Negative Pick-Up Profits." John W. Cones. *Entertainment Law and Finance* 8, no. 3 (June 1992).

Movie Industry Update—1991 (annual publication). Goldman Sachs (Investment Research Report), 1991.

Producing, Financing and Distributing Film—A Comprehensive Legal and Business Guide. 2d ed. Paul A. Baumgarten, Donald C. Farber, and Mark Fleischer. Limelight Editions, 1992.

Reel Power—The Struggle for Influence and Success in the New Hollywood. Mark Litwak. William Morrow, 1986.

"Role of Completion Bonding Companies in Independent Productions." Mark C. Phillips. *Loyola of Los Angeles Entertainment Law* Journal 12, no. 1 (1992).

12

Artificial Pickups

A film project originally controlled and developed by a studio/distributor but which is farmed out pursuant to a negative pickup deal to an outside (but friendly) production company is referred to as an artificial pickup. Artificial pickups are utilized by the studios partly to avoid the higher costs of certain of the below-the-line union crews that the studio may have to pay if the project was produced as an in-house production at the studio or on a production-financing/distribution agreement basis.

A controversial article of the IATSE contract allows major studios to fully finance nonunion movies and television shows so long as the studios declare they have no creative control and give the union thirty days' notice before production starts. Many union supporters contend Article Twenty has helped to increase nonunion movie production. IATSE is the International Alliance of Theatrical and Stage Employees, which in turn is the parent organization of some one thousand local unions in North America representing every branch of film production, including stagehands, makeup artists and wardrobe handlers, as well as employees in film distribution and exhibition.

As reported in the September 14, 1992, *Variety,* "The studios are increasingly pursuing a novel way to cut costs: Develop a picture up to the point of production, then farm it out to an independent producer and call it a negative pickup." The *Variety* story goes on to report that the "studios are routinely doing this on as many as one-third of their releases, especially on lower-budget films [and that] the unions appeared to be going along with the new arrangement. But now there are rumblings of discontent."

The union spokesperson pointed out that "with pickups . . . crew sizes and rates usually are lower [and] indie producers get better union deals than the majors [also the] nonunion shoots pay no health benefits, no pension benefits, no overtime or meal penalties." The article goes on to say that "the majors are all financing pictures through negative pickup deals. They claim no artistic control in the picture and make a distribution deal only . . . we all know they are, in fact, financing non-union work [and] the majors . . . are cutting off thousands of members from their pension and welfare."

Advantages

Studios save money. The artificial pickup allows the studio to make a motion picture (which it developed) for less money than would be required if the film were produced as an in-house production or on a production-financing/distribution basis.

Some producers benefit. The artificial pickup permits independent producers, who might not otherwise be selected by a studio to produce a motion picture, the opportunity to produce a studio-developed film.

Disadvantages

Union relationships. The artificial pickup arrangement is obviously controversial and a producer may be hurting his or her relationships with various unions and guilds by participating in such an arrangement.

Less creative control. Even though a completion guarantor will be required to substitute its monitoring activities and judgment for the assigned studio representative, the producer will still more likely be indebted to the studio for the opportunity to produce the project; thus, the studio's wishes on certain creative issues are less likely to be ignored.

Further Reading

"Cheap Dates Driving New H'wood Pickups." Charles Fleming and Richard Natale. *Variety*, September 14, 1992.

"Entertainment Lending Institutions." *The Hollywood Reporter* (Independent Producers and Distributors Special Report), August 1991.

"Feature Film Secured Financing: A Transactional Approach for Lender's Counsel." Robert G. Weiss and Alan G. Benjamin. *Comm./Ent. L.J.* 5, no. 1 (1982).

Film Finance and Distribution—A Dictionary of Terms. John W. Cones. Silman-James Press, 1992.

Film Industry Contracts. John W. Cones. Self-published, 1993.

"Financing the Production of Theatrical Motion Pictures." Lionel S. Sobel. *Entertainment Law Reporter*, May 1984.

"Hollywood's Family Ways—Who Can You Trust Better Than Kin?" Terry Pristin. *Los Angeles Times* (Calendar section), January 31, 1993.

"Indie Financing Problems Set as Opening Discussion for Santa Monica Confab." Hy Hollinger. *Variety*, February 24, 1992.

"Is the Bond Biz Coming Unglued?" Paul Noglows. *Variety*, April 12, 1993.

"Role of Completion Bonding Companies in Independent Productions." Mark C. Phillips. *Loyola of Los Angeles Entertainment Law Journal* 12, no. 1, (1992).

"Teamsters Uproot Cheapo Shoots." Michael Fleming. *Variety*, October 5, 1992.

13

Presale Financing

Presale financing, in the broadest sense, refers to the funding of a film's production costs through the granting of a license for film rights by a producer to a distributor in a particular media or territory prior to completion of the film. Presales may actually take the form of funds, guarantees or commitments that may be obtained or used to obtain funds, in addition to other available production financing in the form of cash advances or guarantees paid by domestic or foreign distributors, pay or cable television systems, video cassette producers, television syndicators, and/or bank loans obtained by using such cash advances or guarantees as collateral. For example, if a producer had a contract for the presale of a movie to a U.S. or foreign distributor, a home video company, a pay TV service or a TV syndicator, the producer might be able to present those contractual commitments to a bank and walk away with cash (for a fee).

Some speculative numbers. A bank spokesperson has recently estimated that foreign presales are involved in 60 to 65 U.S.-made films each year. According to *Variety*, 436 U.S.-made films were distributed in the domestic theatrical marketplace in 1991, and 417 in 1992; thus, only 14 to 16 percent of the motion pictures released in a given year (or about 1 in 6 or 7 movies) utilize foreign presales.

To the extent that foreign presales are available for a given film, such sales may typically account for as much as 60 percent of a film's budget.

Definitions

Presales. Presales are advance sales of distribution rights in various media and territories.

Presale agreements. In the broadest sense, presale agreements are contracts involving the licensing of feature films that are signed in advance of completion of the film and often in advance of commencement of principal photography. Such agreements may be used

59

by producers to obtain production loans from banks or other lenders (on a discounted basis). In the view of some lenders, the simplest and most desirable form of agreement is the single distribution agreement that covers all rights worldwide or an agreement that is limited to the United States and Canada (domestic territory). That type of arrangement is usually referred to as a negative pickup; thus, a negative pickup is a form of presale.

Fractured-rights deal. A fractured-rights deal is a film finance and distribution transaction, commonly utilized in the 1980s, in which the film's producer (or representative of the producer) presold domestic video and international rights and then engaged a distributor to distribute in the domestic theatrical marketplace for a fee. Sometimes the producer also retained all domestic television rights. The presales would typically cover all of the production costs and some or all of the domestic releasing costs for the picture, leaving the producer's share of theatrical revenues and television rights for potential net profits. Fractured-rights deals worked (1) before video became a significant revenue source for the major studio/distributors (thus, the studios did not demand to participate in the video revenue stream at that time); (2) when independent video companies were still paying substantial fees for video rights, (3) when more banks were prepared to lend money to support these deals and fund production; and (4) when the funds supplied by independent video companies and outside banks were sufficient to cover production costs and a significant portion of domestic releasing costs. The fractured-rights deals of the 1980s have now been replaced by the so-called split-rights deals.

Split-rights deal. The split-rights deal is a film financing and distribution transaction, which has apparently replaced the fractured-rights deals of the 1980s, in which the producer presells all domestic rights to a distributor and retains international rights. By keeping the international rights on a promising film that is prepackaged and financed, the producer may be able to sell the international rights on an auction basis to the highest bidder. The total price obtained may exceed the actual costs incurred in making the film. In addition, the domestic and international rights are not cross-collateralized (i.e., they are uncrossed) with respect to the producer. In the event that the film is well received at the box office either in the domestic marketplace or internationally, the producer may earn more overages than in a crossed situation, such as a worldwide negative pickup or P-F/D deal. The producer may also be able to limit the studio/distributor's term of rights in split-rights deals, insuring that the film ultimately becomes an addition to the producer's library of films, not the distributor's.

Note that lenders do not consider the distribution agreement alone a presale contract. In their view, in order to be a presale contract, that is, one that is lendable, the contract must guarantee the payment of a specific amount of money by a certain date, and a distribution agreement alone (as opposed to a distribution agreement with a guarantee) only provides that the distributor will distribute the film to exhibitors.

A feature film's distribution rights as to separate media may be fractionalized and presold pursuant to separate agreements relating to video rights, pay television rights, theatrical rights, U.S. network television rights and possibly even local television syndication rights. In addition, presales may be negotiated for foreign territories and in fact may begin with the foreign territories.

Presales Used to Finance Production Costs

The role of the sales agent. The producer typically contracts with an experienced sales agent to make presale arrangements on behalf of a film. Such responsibilities may be divided among domestic and foreign sales agents (see *Know your buyer* below).

What the producer gets. The sales agent may be able to obtain a 10 to 20 percent cash deposit at the time of signing the presale agreement and will seek to obtain a minimum guarantee payable upon delivery of the motion picture to the buyer. The sales agent typically will get a presales agreement that is sometimes backed by the presales purchasing entity's letter of credit or other form of financial guarantee (e.g., a guaranty provided by a financially sound third party to insure payment of foreign contracts provided by foreign distributors who are not considered financially strong by the lender). In the above example, the producer may be required to assign a portion of the picture's net profits to the guarantor for providing the guaranty; however, that eliminates one of the big selling points for using a loan for production funds.

The producer then goes to the lender. The producer then may be able to take the presales agreement to a bank or other lender and use it in conjunction with distribution agreements and guarantees, other presale agreements or other forms of collateral to obtain a production loan, which may cover the cost of producing the film or may be used in conjunction with other financing sources (e.g., investor funds) or other financing techniques (e.g., deferrals, government subsidies, etc.) to produce the film. The producer will try to borrow money by pledging the presale agreement itself. However, many U.S. banks will not discount (i.e., lend against) foreign paper. In the alternative the producer may be required to obtain letters of credit from the foreign buyer. A letter of credit is generally considered more bankable than a contract to pay the same amount of money.

The lender's judgment. A lender will make an independent judgment as to whether to lend on a given presale agreement, based on the reputation and track record of the presale purchasing entity and the terms of the agreement itself. A letter of credit put up by the presale purchasing entity would provide the lender with additional security and make it more likely that the lender would be able to lend on the presale agreement.

Discounting. Once the bank has determined (through weight analysis) the loan amount, it then discounts that loan amount to arrive at sums allocated for the production of the film, a production contingency, loan fees, bank legal fees and interest. The bank sets up a production account and a reserve account (from which to pay all items other than the production monies).

The investor alternative. The producer does not always have to take the presale agreements to lenders but may opt for using such presale agreements as a means of reducing the downside risk for investors in an investor-financed film project. Thus, if for any reason, the presales contracts are not considered lendable by lenders (banks and other lending institutions), the producer may want to consider investor-financing alternatives.

Sales agent fees. Sales agent fees may range from approximately 10 to 15 percent if the sales agent is not able to negotiate any form of guarantee from the presale purchasing entity (such as an irrevocable letter of credit), but with some form of financial guarantee provided by the presales purchasing entity, the sales agent's fees may increase to as high as 30 percent. Cash payments, either at the signing stage or as an advance payable upon delivery, may also tend to increase the sales agent's fees.

Issues that may be negotiated. The prospective quality of the picture (i.e., the strength of the package), along with the competitive environment and the general demand (or lack thereof) for product in a given market, will help determine whether the sales agent is able to successfully negotiate on behalf of a producer's film. Questions relating to what rights are included, the film's genre (e.g., action/adventure or comedy), censorship, price ceilings imposed by local industries, the amount of deposits paid by the buyer to the sales agent on behalf of the film producer, minimum guarantees to be paid on delivery of the picture and back-end participation will typically be considered in such negotiations.

A presale strategy. The producer should try to retain as many rights and territories for sale after completion of the motion picture as possible, that is, presell only as many rights and territories as necessary to cover the production costs of the picture.

The role of hype. Some suggest that the desire of the distributors to distribute a film is to some extent based on industry hype, for example, announcements in the trades, and that such hype, typically generated through the efforts of a professional publicist, contributes to a certain level of presumed value for the film among the distributors.

When to approach sales agents. Obviously, the earlier the producer establishes lines of communication with a reputable sales agent, the better, since those early conversations with the sales agent who is presumably out there on the front lines of the marketplace on a daily basis may result in valuable guidance to the producer in developing and packaging the film. Ultimately, the sales agent will need a fairly complete packaged film project before the sales agent will be taken seriously by potential presales purchasing entities. Thus, a completed and budgeted script along with commitments from a director and "marquee" actors constitute the minimum package with which the sales agent can work. Of course, it also helps if the producer, coproducer or executive producer associated with the project has a reputation for having delivered commercial films in the past. The strength of the writer of the screenplay will also add value to the package.

Know your buyer. The producer will, as a practical matter, have to rely on the judgment of the sales agent, but it is critical that the sales agent know how many films the prospective presale purchasing entity (buyer) licenses in a year, whether the buyer is well financed and whether the buyer has defaulted on a presale agreement in the past. Favorable information relating to these questions may decrease the likelihood of the default disaster discussed below. Obtaining letters of credit would also help alleviate the problems of a buyer default.

Some financing in place. Part of the financing for producing a motion picture must be in place before presales can be attempted. In other words, at a minimum, the screenplay must have already been acquired or be under option to the producer, and that typically involves an up-front out-of-pocket expense for the producer. In addition, if not pay-or-play, some payments are likely to have been required in order to obtain commitments from the director and actors.

The producer's package. From a presentation point of view, the producer needs to work closely with the sales agent in developing an attractive physical package that the sales agent may use in presenting the project to prospective presale purchasing entities. Such a package may include glossy photos of committed actors and actresses, their credits and/or narrative biographies, the letters of intent or interest of such persons, a synopsis of the screenplay, the director's credits/biography, similar information on other committed personnel and the producer, the projected cost of producing the film, location information, press clippings relating to those involved in the project, information relating to any existing distribution or presale agreements and so forth.

Drafting Checklist for Presale Agreements

Objective delivery. The completion guarantor and producer will not want the distributor to be able to avoid its advance payment obligations once delivery is made. Thus, the delivery schedule and obligations of the producer must be drafted as objectively as possible.

Script approval. The distributor will generally want an approval right, that is, the ability to sign off on a specific final draft of the screenplay. However, in drafting that provision in the distribution negative pickup agreement, some flexibility should be provided for the producer in anticipation of required script changes that fall within a reasonable range of directorial creativity and changes that are prompted by unavoidable problems that may occur while shooting the film.

Specified MPAA rating. Generally, the distributor will require that the producer commit to provide a film with a specific MPAA rating, for example, an R rating. The producer and director must carefully weigh the risk of not being able to provide a particular rating for a movie based on the subject screenplay, since failure to comply with that requirement may allow the distributor to refuse to distribute the film, that is, avoid its obligations under a negative pickup distribution agreement.

Television cover shots. Typically the distributor will ask that the producer commit in the distribution agreement to provide a version of the film that is suitable for broadcast on U.S. free television. This may be difficult, since each of the free television networks in the United States has a separate standards and practices department that passes on the content of feature films to be aired on its network. Some feature films (particularly R-rated films) do not meet the networks' more restrictive standards. Thus, the producer should agree to provide cover shots that are more likely to meet the network standards and should require the distributor to designate in advance scenes for which it will require television cover shots.

Production versus distribution expenses. The producer should carefully review the long list of delivery items that is often part of a long-form distribution agreement and seek to eliminate items that should more properly be characterized as a distributor responsibility and therefore a distributor expense as opposed to items that are paid for out of the film's production budget. If an item is something the distributor is responsible for and therefore a distributor expense, it will generally be recouped as a distributor expense. On the other hand, if such an item is improperly characterized as a production expense, that is, treated as part of the cost of the negative, interest will be paid on the cost of such item until the bank loan is repaid. A higher total interest cost can thus result.

Running time requirements. The producer's counsel should also watch for an unduly restrictive ceiling on the running time for the film, since an arbitrary limit may saddle a producer and director with an unsatisfactory creative result or, in the alternative, provide the distributor with grounds for refusing to distribute the picture.

Negotiations of the issues discussed above, which tend to increase the likelihood that a film will be accepted by the distributor, will increase the receptiveness of a lender to lend production funds based on a presale agreement and guarantee. When presale contracts (with guarantees) form the collateral for a loan, the lender must determine that the collateral and the transaction are lendable.

Advantages

Presales may raise a significant portion of production financing. As an example, the discounted value of foreign presales (which typically include video and television rights for that territory) may equal 40 to 60 percent of a film's production budget. Approximately 85 percent of the foreign territorial sales of American films (not just presold rights) come from eight of the forty countries that typically distribute U.S.-made films. Those eight most important foreign territories (listed by market share and assuming that Canada is part of the domestic market) are Japan, France, Germany, Britain/Ireland, Spain, Italy, Australia and Sweden.

Less studio creative intervention. From a creative point of view, providing financing for a feature film through presales reduces what in many instances is a problem for some producers and directors, that is, the oversight and interference of a major studio/distributor in the production process. However, lenders will require that a completion bond be provided, and the completion guarantor will generally have its representative actively monitoring the production. If problems occur, the completion guarantor's representative will become very involved in day-to-day decisions that impact on the budget, and it is difficult to separate budget decisions from creative decisions. Thus, discounted presales involving loans do not necessarily permit the kind of creative control so important to many producers and directors; that is, much of the studio intervention is merely replaced with intervention by the completion guarantor.

No other production financing options may be open. If a producer cannot obtain studio production financing, a production-financing/distribution deal from other distributors, a negative pickup deal with a guarantee sufficient to interest lenders, or other collateral besides presales satisfactory to lenders or investor financing in some form (e.g., a limited partnership), then the producer who is determined to make a film has little choice but to resort to fractionalizing or splitting media and territories and preselling some of those to generate lendable contracts to raise production financing through loans.

No confidence in the upside. If a producer does not really have confidence in the economic upside potential of the picture about to be produced, presales make even more sense. And since very few motion pictures are big box-office successes at any level, how can any producer be that confident of the upside potential of a given film? Furthermore, since most producers do not generally participate in the upside potential of their own films, the loss of the financial upside does not become a disadvantage for producers. On the other hand, producers must include those factors in their analysis of the value of their motion picture when making the original deal with the distributor.

From the buyer's perspective. Through presale agreements, the prospective presale purchasing entity (licensee or buyer) hopes to secure the rights to exploit good films before a competitor has had a chance to license the same motion picture.

Disadvantages

Collection difficulties. Presales are based on contingencies, for example, the actual collection of moneys due from the providers of presale contracts, and have turned out to be difficult in some instances.

Increased P&A costs make presales less practical. Fractionalized and split-rights agreements have become less practical in recent years because of the increasing relative cost of U.S. theatrical distribution, including paid advertising and film prints.

Domestic presales may eliminate certain distributors. U.S. theatrical distributors often insist upon all or substantially all rights to help cover recoupment not only of advances to the producer but also their increased distribution costs. That is, any ancillary right that has significant value will be demanded by the domestic theatrical distributor as a prerequisite of distribution. Thus, the producer who presells a film's cable and video rights runs the risk of preselling the film out of a domestic theatrical release. And since the cable and video presale contracts will probably require a domestic theatrical release at a specified level (e.g., number of theatres), if there is no domestic theatrical release, then both the cable and video agreements are likely to be voided.

Counterargument. If a producer produces a film that every studio/distributor or independent distributor wants to distribute, then presales may not interfere with the producer's ability to obtain a domestic theatrical release. Ultimately, the quality of the finished film will determine, to some extent, whether presales will preclude a domestic theatrical release.

Cost-value trends do not favor fractionalized presales. As film production and distribution costs have increased, the percentage of revenue generated through a film's domestic theatrical release has been reduced in relation to other media or territories and the value of cable and video rights has increased, domestic theatrical distributors have been more likely to insist on requiring the domestic cable and video rights as part of any domestic theatrical distribution deal.

Theatrical release creates value in ancillary markets. The domestic theatrical distributors point out that their expenditures on prints, ads and publicity helps to create value for a film in the other markets; thus, in all fairness, they should be allowed to participate in those markets.

More offers means less reason to presell. The more value a film is presumed to have, the higher the offers distributors and ancillary buyers are willing to make to keep their competition from buying the same rights. But the more offers the producer gets for ancillary rights, the more confident the producer can be that the film actually has value and that all rights can subsequently be sold to an important distributor.

Gives away upside potential. Film production companies relying on presale strategies may succeed in reducing but not eliminating their downside risk, while giving away much of a film's upside potential.

Presales bring lower prices. The price that a buyer is willing to pay before seeing a prospective film will generally be less than that which the same buyer would pay for the same film as a completed motion picture; thus, the upside potential is reduced. This means that production companies relying entirely on a presale strategy will have a difficult time surviving on a long-term basis.

The "A" picture dilemma. Many industry observers today suggest that it is difficult to presell rights in major markets around the world without an extremely strong film package, the so-called A picture. On the other hand, if a producer has an A picture, why should it be necessary to seek presales? Furthermore, the stronger motion picture package will generally require more money to finance; therefore, more presales will have to be made.

Higher cost of capital. Companies relying on presales will inevitably have a relatively high cost of capital compared to some other forms of film finance. For example, in a foreign territory presale, a sales agent's fee will typically be recouped in addition to the costs and fees of the foreign distributor before the producer will receive payments, if any, beyond the producer's advance.

Takes too much time. Since it generally takes much more time to contact and negotiate with multiple interested buyers of presold rights in the various media and territories, producers using presales may encounter a lengthier time lag between the start of production and the creation of library asset values on films produced and distributed through presale arrangements than some other forms of film finance.

Contractual quagmire. From a contractual point of view, it is difficult to coordinate the various contractual concerns of the bank, the completion bond companies, the producer and the various media and territories when negotiating and drafting multiple presale agreements.

Reversion rights and library values. When preselling rights to a film in various markets and media, the production company or its attorney must be careful to coordinate provisions relating to the reversion of such rights to the producer following exploitation of the film in such markets and media. If not, the film is likely to have less value as a library asset, and confusion over the status of such rights may make it difficult to include such film in the sale of a production company's film library.

Default disaster. If a licensee (i.e., the presales purchasing entity or buyer) sees a rough cut of the film and decides it is so much worse than expected (or otherwise unsatisfactory), the buyer may notify the producer that it will not be paying the balance of the minimum guarantee and will forfeit its deposit, if any. In that event, the bank may demand that the producer repay the loan, and the producer may have to seek payment from the distributor. If the producer fails to repay the loan, the bank might foreclose on the negative if it took a lien as further collateral or attach the film and its proceeds even if it did not have an original lien.

Survival of the weakest. Presales often support projects that perhaps could not and should not otherwise have been made; thus, producers seeking presale commitments may be looked upon with disfavor in some segments of the industry.

The long-term view. Over the long term, the relatively few films that are highly profitable for a producer using presale strategies are likely to be insufficient in number or in degree of success to recoup the losses of the firm's many nonprofitable projects. In other words, the thinner potential profit margins of presold films make it less likely that such a production company will financially succeed in the long run.

Macroeconomics. Feature films financed in this manner increase the number of films produced in a given year and thereby increase the demand for, and thus the cost of, various film elements that are theoretically in limited supply (e.g., screenplays, directors, actors, sound stages, etc.). Also, since there are more films produced each year than there are capable and willing distributors available to distribute, the oversupply of films contributes to a significant imbalance in the bargaining strength between producers and distributors.

Further Reading

"Banks, Investors Still Shy on Indies." Linda Keslar. *Variety,* November 16, 1992.

The Business of Show Business: Legal Affairs for the Independent Producer. Beverly Hills Bar Association Entertainment Law Section (half-day workshop at ShowBiz Expo). Produced by Bruce Kassman, 1992.

"CBC RIP: Independents Lose Their Biggest Backer." Paul Noglows. *Daily Variety,* June 1, 1992.

"Could Lender Bender Land Bank in Tank?" Judy Brennan. *Variety,* January 11, 1993.

"Entertainment Financing for the '90s: Super Pre-Sales." Schuyler M. Moore. Stroock and Stroock and Lavan, *Corporate Entertainment Newsletter* 1, Q1 (1992).

Entertainment Industry Economics: A Guide for Financial Analysis. 2d ed. Harold L. Vogel. Cambridge University Press, 1990.

"Entertainment Lending Institutions." *The Hollywood Reporter,* Independent Producers and Distributors Special Report, August 1991.

"Feature Film Secured Financing: A Transactional Approach for Lender's Counsel." Robert G. Weiss and Alan G. Benjamin. *Comm./Ent. L.J.* 5, no. 1 (1982).

Film and Video Financing. Michael Wiese. Michael Wiese Productions, 1991.

Film Finance and Distribution—A Dictionary of Terms. John W. Cones. Silman-James Press, 1992.

"Film Financing Makes a Turn to the Rights." Kim Masters. *Los Angeles Daily News,* p. 1, July 18, 1987.

Film Industry Contracts. John W. Cones. Self-published, 1993.

"Financing Independent Films—Wall Street Funding May Be Drying Up, But New Opportunities Beckon from Europe and the Far East." Bruce St. J Lilliston. *Los Angeles Lawyer,* p. 19, May 1988.

"The Financing of Independent Motion Pictures in 1989." Peter J. Dekom. *American Premiere,* 1989.

"Financing the Production of Theatrical Motion Pictures." Lionel S. Sobel. *Entertainment Law Reporter,* May 1984.

Financing Your Film—A Guide for Independent Filmmakers and Producers. Trisha Curran. Praeger Publishers, 1986.

"Finding a Formula to Finance Indies." Scott Young. *The Hollywood Reporter,* January 25, 1991.

"H'wood Rights Make Euro Might." Richard Natale. *Variety,* August 31, 1992.

"Indie Financing Problems Set as Opening Discussion for Santa Monica Confab." Hy Hollinger. *Variety,* February 24, 1992.

"Is the Bond Biz Coming Unglued?" Paul Noglows. *Variety,* April 12, 1993.

Legal Aspects of Film Financing. Rick Barsky, Noreena Hertz, George Ros, and Jonathan L. Vinnik, Self-published, April 1990.

"Making Millions and Going Broke—How Production Companies Make Fortunes and Bankrupt Themselves." David Royal. *American Premiere*, November/December 1991.

"New Player Swinging in Film Finance Ring." Don Groves. *Variety*, p. 259, October 14, 1991.

"One Producer's Inside View of Foreign and Domestic Pre-Sales in the Independent Financing of Motion Pictures." Arnold Kopelson. *Loyola of Los Angeles Entertainment Law Journal*, 1992.

"Pic Banker Afman Joints ICM to Run New Finance Unit." Andrea King. *The Hollywood Reporter*, p. 3, July 12, 1991.

"Pick-Ups, Pre-Sales and Co-Ventures." P. J. Abode. *Montage* (IFP/West publication), Winter 1991/1992.

Producing, Financing and Distributing Film—A Comprehensive Legal and Business Guide. 2d ed. Paul A. Baumgarten, Donald C. Farber, and Mark Fleischer. Limelight Editions, 1992.

"The Recondite Discountable-Contract Finance: An Elucidation of Negative-Pickup and Presale Financing Arrangements." Jeff Foy. *Beverly Hills Bar Association Journal* 27, no. 1 (Winter, 1993).

"Role of Completion Bonding Companies in Independent Productions." Mark C. Phillips. *Loyola of Los Angeles Entertainment Law Journal* 12, no. 1 (1992).

"Strategies for the International Production and Distribution of Feature Films in the 1990's." Thomas J. Cryan, David W. Johnson, James S. Crane, and Anthony Cammarata. *Loyola Entertainment Law Journal* 8 (1988).

PART 3

Investor Financing

14

The Self-funded Sole Proprietorship

In the context of film finance, the sole proprietorship is the simplest and usually the first form of doing business for the producer's production company. The sole proprietorship is an unincorporated production company owned and managed by one person, for the purpose of making a profit. Out-of-pocket start-up expenses are often paid for by the sole owner.

Generally, it will be necessary for the owner of a film production company organized as a sole proprietorship to file a Fictitious Business Name Statement (in California) or to effect an *assumed name* filing (in other states) if the name under which the business is being conducted is different from the name of the individual owner. In some jurisdictions this form of doing business is referred to as a *dba*, that is, "doing business as" (name of company).

At least initially, the film production company organized as a sole proprietorship will generally be self-funded by the individual owner; however, the self-funded sole proprietorship may also seek loans, use an investor financing agreement, the investment contract or serve as the general partner of a limited partnership for subsequent development and/or production funds.

Advantages

Creative control. The owner of a production company operating as a sole proprietorship has the authority to ultimately make all of the creative and other decisions regarding the operations of the company. In other words, there is only one boss and conflicts are thus minimized.

Self-reliance. The sole proprietor is not subject to the incompetence, mismanagement or fraud of others who may have to be relied on in conjunction with other forms of doing business.

Cannot be fired. The sole proprietor of a film production company cannot be fired or otherwise removed from his or her office.

Few legal formalities. There are few, if any, legal formalities that need be followed in creating the sole proprietorship except that if the production company is operating under a name other than the name of the individual owner, the company needs to effect a fictitious name filing with the county clerk in the county in which the firm is doing business (also called an *assumed name* filing in some states) and possibly with the secretary of state in some states.

No formal maintenance requirements. There are also no formal maintenance requirements as in a corporation, such as the holding of annual shareholder meetings, the calling of regular meetings of a board of directors, the maintenance of minutes of such meetings or the approval of board resolutions for significant company actions.

Inheritance. A film production company organized as a sole proprietorship can be left to the individual owner's heirs with or without a will.

Selling the business. The owner of a film production company organized as a sole proprietorship can sell the business or its assets (e.g., films produced or equipment) without the approval of or negotiations with partners or other owners.

Taxation. The income of the sole proprietorship is taxed as the personal income of the individual owner at individual rates as opposed to corporate rates. Thus, depending on the current state of the tax laws, it may be taxed at a lower rate.

Disadvantages

Start-up costs. The owner of a film production company organized as a sole proprietorship may have to bear the burden of start-up costs.

Only decision maker. In some instances, being the only decision maker can be a burden.

Raising funds. It is generally more difficult to raise funds from investors, using this form of doing business.

Personal liability. The owner of the film production company organized as a sole proprietorship is personally liable for the obligations of the business and its debts.

Tax deductions. The unincorporated sole proprietor cannot deduct losses from passive income, write off medical expenses or deduct the cost of pension plans, while, under current tax provisions, a corporation can do so.

Difficult to sell. A film production company organized as a sole proprietorship may be more difficult to sell than a production company organized as a corporation since the most important asset of the sole proprietorship is often its owner.

Doing business with others. Many businesses prefer to do business with corporations as opposed to sole proprietorships.

Key employees. It is more difficult to entice key employees to work for a sole proprietorship and to create profit-sharing arrangements.

Further Reading

California Corporate Practice Guide 2d. Morgan D. King. Lawpress Corporation, 1989.

Feature Filmmaking at Used-Car Prices—How to Write, Produce, Direct, Film, Edit, and Promote a Feature-Length Film for Less than $10,000. Rick Schmidt. Penguin paperback.

Feature Films on a Low Budget. John Randall. Focal Press, 1991.

Film Finance and Distribution—A Dictionary of Terms. John W. Cones. Silman-James Press, 1992.

Film Industry Contracts. John W. Cones. Self-published, 1993.

The Partnership Book. Denis Clifford and Ralph Warner. Nolo Press, 1988.

Small Time Operator. Bernard Kamoroff. Bell Springs.

15

Business Plans

Technically speaking, the business plan is not a financing vehicle or entity but can be used in conjunction with several other investor-financing techniques to raise money for film projects. For example, a business plan can be used with an investor-financing agreement to raise money from a single active investor. It can be used with a joint venture agreement to raise money from another entity also acting as an active investor/joint venture partner. It can also be used as a means of identifying possible founding shareholders for the initial incorporation, a strategy discussed elsewhere in this book (see chapter 18).

Another important use of the business plan is helpful in establishing a preexisting relationship with prospective investors for a subsequent securities offering (see chapters 19–25). Thus, the business plan becomes a method for conducting a general solicitation while looking for active investors (see chapter 16), and if the active investor campaign does not prove successful, then the campaign can be converted into a securities offering (seeking passive investors). If the *private placement* approach is used for the subsequent securities offering, those persons contacted during the active investor general solicitation (using the business plan) may be approached as prospective investors for the private placement since the initial contact with those prospective investors is likely to be sufficient to establish the preexisting relationship, which, although not technically required by the federal securities laws, still is an important element in proving that no general solicitation occurred.

The film production company business plan can be very similar to the producer's package except that it is usually bound and may be presented in a more organized fashion. The business plan is often the first step in procuring investor financing, whereas the producer's package is used for similar purposes in obtaining funding from a distributor or other industry source. The producer's package might include, for example, a screenplay, a list of credits for key persons attached to the project and a proposed budget, whereas a business plan might include a synopsis of the screenplay, narrative biographies of the key persons attached to the project and a use of proceeds section, which corresponds closely to the budget top sheet. A business plan can be as simple or as sophisticated as the producer and his or her advisers choose to make it.

Since, as a practical matter, the use of a business plan is limited to raising small amounts of money, in addition to serving as a means of financing for ultra-low budget feature films, it may be quite useful for funding the development stage of a film project. For example, a producer may want to incorporate his or her production company with five or six of the producer's closest advisor/investors (let's say raising $50,000 at $10,000 each from five founding shareholder investor friends or family) for the purpose of financing the costs associated with acquisition, development, packaging and preproduction. This corporate production company could then subsequently serve as the corporate general partner for a film limited partnership created for the purpose of funding the production stage of the film. Other development stage/business plan scenarios involving the investor-financing agreement, the joint venture and even an active-investor liability company could be utilized.

The following is a sample outline of a business plan to be used in promoting a feature film production company:

Business Plan
  Executive Summary
  Introduction (Setting of the Stage)
  Status of the Independent Producer
  General Company Description
  Management and Organization (narrative biographies)
  The Proposed Film
    Film Synopsis/Treatment
    Screenplay Rights
    Comparable Box Office Performances (or distributor rentals)
    Production of the Picture
    Budget/Use of Proceeds
    Distribution Approach
    Funding of the Picture and Cofinancing
Industry Overview
Exhibits
  Résumés of Principals

Literary Property Option/Acquisition Agreements
Financial Statement
Letters of Interest/Intent
Industry Articles
Press Coverage
Financial Projections

The following are other possible exhibits (depending on the stage at which financing is sought) that may be included as part of the business plan: title report, copyright search report, chain of title documents including a certificate of authorship for the screenplay, copy of the copyright registration, copyright assignment, distribution agreement(s), completion bond commitment letter, corporate resolution authorizing the producer to negotiate and sign a financing agreement, final screenplay and shooting script, cast and production credits, synopsis of the script, biographies of key people, feature stories on lead actors and the director, production stills, casual cast photos, agreements relating to the film's music, the MPAA ratings certificate (if available) and the E&O certificate of insurance.

Advantages

No securities laws involved. So long as the business plan is associated with an active investor form of financing (i.e., investor-financing agreement, joint venture or initial incorporation—see chapters 16–18), producers using a business plan may approach any prospective investor without fear of violating the securities law prohibitions relating to private placements, which in turn (as a practical matter) limit offers and sales to persons with whom the producer or other upper-level management of the issuing entity have a preexisting relationship.

No formal rules. There are no formal rules promulgated by any governmental authority regulating the contents of a business plan; thus, producers have considerable freedom in drafting such a document. There still may be some liability, however, for inaccurate or misleading statements.

Relatively easy to assemble. In the context of the film business, a business plan is merely a specific adaptation of the producer's package, which in turn contains many of the documents a producer would ordinarily generate in the preplanning stages of putting together a film project.

General solicitation permitted. The business plan, properly handled, allows the producer to go out into the marketplace and conduct a general solicitation for a single active investor or other possible combinations, and if not successful in raising the necessary moneys using the business plan, the producer may convert his or her offering into a securities offering and then go back and call on those same investors within the context of a securities private placement.

Disadvantages

May be unneeded step. If the producer already knows that he or she is going to use the limited partnership as the financing vehicle, for example, and already has a sufficient pool of prospective investors available, the business plan is just another step in the financing process that might be eliminated.

Inadvertent securities sales. Producers who are not aware of the important distinction between active and passive investor offerings may confuse the two in using a business plan and thus inadvertently be guilty of selling an unregistered security. Thus, producers beware: ignorance of the law is no excuse.

Further Reading

The Ernst and Young Business Plan Guide. Eric S. Siegel, Loren A. Schultz, Brian R. Ford, and David C. Carney. John Wiley & Sons, 1987.

Feature Films on a Low Budget. John Randall. Focal Press, 1991.

Film Finance and Distribution—A Dictionary of Terms. John W. Cones. Silman-James Press, 1992.

"Tide of H'wood Investment Rising—Stock Offerings Buoy Industry to the Tune of $3.24 Billion." Robert Marich and Jeffrey Daniels. *The Hollywood Reporter,* August 15, 1991.

16

The Investor-Financing Agreement

The investor-financing agreement is one of several active investor-financing techniques. The other two discussed in this book are the joint venture and the initial incorporation. The investor-financing agreement is merely a contractual arrangement between the film's producer and a single active investor. The single active investor makes whatever contributions to the project that are agreed upon and set forth in the contract in exchange for screen credit and a percentage participation at some specified level of the film's revenue stream, for example, 50 percent of the producer's share of net profits or 25 percent of the film's net proceeds.

Use with business plan. Just as with the initial incorporation and the joint venture, the investor-financing agreement may be used in conjunction with a business plan to offer a single active investor an opportunity to review the business plan for a given film project or film production company and then to immediately invest by signing the accompanying investor-financing agreement and submitting his or her check to the producer.

Active investor. The investor-financing agreement should specifically set out how the investor is going to be involved in the management of the project. In other words, in order to be considered active, the investor must materially participate in the activity; that is, the investor must be involved in the film's operations on a sufficiently regular, continuous and substantial basis. Not only must the investor-financing agreement describe the level of investor involvement, but the investor's actual conduct must reflect that active involvement, and it is important that the producer develop documentary evidence tending to show such involvement on the part of the investor.

The investor-financing agreement, which typically might be six to seven pages in length, might, as an example, include the following headings and subheadings:

The Picture and Production Arrangements
Distribution of the Picture
Recoupment of Investment; Percentage Share of Profits
    Recoupment and Interest—Priority Payments
    Net Profit Participation
    Third-Party Net Profit Participations
Investor's Monetary Contribution
Investor Approval Rights
Budget
Return of Unexpended Contributions
Representations and Warranties
    Powers and Authority
    Legal Validity
    Nonconflict with Laws
    Consents
    Litigation
    Copy Documents
    Material Information
    Survival
Indemnification by Production Company
Accounting and Reports by Production Company
Funds Held in Trust
Relationship of Parties
Business Opportunities
Additional Documents
Notices
Assignment
Miscellaneous
    Amendments
    No Third-Party Beneficiary Contract
    No Continuing Waiver
    Applicable Law
    Arbitration
    Attorney's Fees
    Entire Agreement

Agreements like the investor-financing agreement may be called by another name. For example, if the agreement is actually being used to raise development money, it may be referred to as a Development Money Investor Agreement or something similar to that. It is important to recognize, however, that even if the money being raised is to be used only for acquisition and/or development purposes, the critical distinction relating to securities law compliance is whether the investor is passive or active. As a general rule, passive investors invest in securities; active investors invest in nonsecurities.

Advantages

Simplest form of investor financing. The investor-financing agreement may be the simplest form of investor financing and therefore the least expensive.

Works with business plan. The investor-financing agreement can be provided to prospective investors along with the business plan so that if the prospective active investor is impressed with the business plan and wants to invest, he or she may do so through the investor-financing agreement.

Disadvantages

Single investor. It is not always easy to find a single investor who has the wherewithal to fund the entire production budget for a motion picture, even a low-budget film.

Multiple investors. To the extent that the producer may want to add a few active investors, he or she must realize that the more investors there are, the less likely that all of them will be truly active investors. Thus, the chances are increased that the producer has actually raised money from one or more passive investors, which probably means that the securities laws are involved and compliance with such laws would be required.

Active investor. In order to avoid having to comply with the federal and state securities laws, the producer must make certain that the investor is actively involved in the making of management decisions on a regular basis.

Further Reading

Entertainment Industry Contracts—Negotiating and Drafting Guide. Donald C. Farber, Jay S. Kenoff, and Richard K. Rosenberg. Matthew Bender, 1991.

Feature Films on a Low Budget. John Randall. Focal Press, 1991.

Film Finance and Distribution—A Dictionary of Terms. John W. Cones. Silman-James Press, 1992.

Film Industry Contracts. John W. Cones. Self-published, 1993.

17

Joint-Venture Financing

The following summary discussion of the joint-venture-financing vehicle seeks to distinguish the joint venture from similar forms of film finance and to highlight some of the more important issues that arise when using this vehicle.

Joint venture versus general partnership. A joint venture is a specialized form of general partnership, created for a limited purpose; that is, its scope is limited. A general partnership, on the other hand, is used when the active investors intend to establish a continuing business relationship devoted to a broadly defined purpose or purposes.

Joint venture versus limited partnership. Generally, the joint venture will be used when the investors are fewer in number and financially knowledgeable, but, even more important, they must all be active investors, that is, actively involved in the project. In contrast, the limited partnership investors must be passive investors. Thus, some aspects of the advantage of producer creative control, which the limited partnership offers, may be lost with the joint venture. Also, the limited partnership offers its investors limited liability, whereas the joint venture does not. The joint venture would be most appropriate when one entity provides the financing, the other entity brings the literary property and talent to the deal, and both are to be actively involved in the management of the project.

Joint venture versus investor-financing agreement. Generally, an investor-financing agreement may be used when a single active investor is providing all of the funds to finance the production costs of a motion picture (which may also be the case with a joint venture). However, the investor-financing agreement merely involves a contractual arrangement between the investor and the production company. No separate entity, as with the joint venture, is created.

No limited liability. Under applicable law, general partnerships and joint ventures are treated the same. Both are general partnerships in that joint venturers have the same liability that general partners have under the law of partnerships, that is, joint and several.

Joint venturer contributions. In the context of financing a feature film or films, the joint venture usually consists of two or more companies that contribute various elements to the project, some of which may be nonmonetary, such as unequal responsibilities, the script or underlying property, commitments from a director or actors, below-the-line facilities, and the like. In other words, one joint venturer may contribute some or all of the money, and the other joint venturer may contribute the packaged literary property. The contributions of limited partners in a limited partnership, on the other hand, are generally monetary, even though some of the state laws regulating such contributions permit limited partners to contribute money, property and/or past services (not future services). The major distinction still is how actively involved in the project the money partners can be.

Creative control issue. In negotiating and drafting a joint venture agreement, one of the most important issues is creative control. The joint venturer contributing the creative elements will typically want to maintain as much creative control as possible. The joint venturer contributing all or most of the financing for the project may want to have some important input relating to creative matters; thus, specific provisions need to be set out on this issue, for example, approval rights.

Duration of the joint venture. The term of the motion picture joint venture will generally be expressed in the alternative, for example, for a short specified term if production financing is not obtained, for the longest term of any of the agreements relating to the literary property or for the duration of any and all copyrights owned by the joint venture.

Title to the property. Usually, the literary property is transferred into the joint venture and a provision is included that specifies that all rights to the literary property are held in the name of the joint venture. If, on the other hand, the joint venture does not hold title to the literary property, but merely acquires some more limited rights to the property, the joint venturer contributing most or all of the money may want to create a security interest in the literary property to help assure performance by the other joint venturer of its obligations under the joint venture agreement.

Allocation of profits and losses. Like the general and limited partnerships, the profits and losses of the joint venture pass through to the joint venturers; thus, the joint venture itself is not a taxable entity. The joint venturers are free to allocate profits, losses, tax credits and deductions in whatever manner suits them. Such decisions may be changed and modified at any time before the due date of the federal informational return for that taxable year.

Books, records and bank account. Provision must be made for the creation and maintenance of books, records and a bank account for the joint venture, for naming the person responsible for such activities and for securing access to such by the other joint venturer.

Resolving disputes. Since it is vital to keep a motion picture project moving forward without undue delay, it is extremely important to include a provision in the joint venture agreement relating to how disputes that arise between the joint venturers can be quickly resolved. They can agree either that one of the joint venturers will have the final say-so on certain specified issues or that a third party or third parties will resolve such differences.

Tax consequences. Like a limited partnership, a joint venture must normally file an informational tax return. Certain tax elections, for example, methods of depreciation, affecting the computation of a joint venturer's taxable income must be made by the joint venture itself. A joint venture must adopt its own taxable year, but it may not adopt a taxable year different from that of any principal partner without the consent of the IRS. Tax issues may also arise when each of the joint venturers makes different contributions of money and property, for example, who is credited with the depreciation on contributed property and who receives any capital gain or loss allocations.

Other issues and provisions. Additional provisions of the joint venture agreement may relate to management responsibilities of the parties, screen credit, distribution of available cash, joint venturer involvement in other similar projects at the same time, indemnification and warranty requirements, procedures in the event of the death or disability of a joint venturer, dissolution and termination of the joint venture, notices, arbitration and so forth.

Sample Joint Venture Agreement Outline

Date of Agreement
Name of Joint Venturers
  1. Purpose
  2. Term
  3. Name and Statutory Compliance
  4. Title

  5. Principal Office
  6. Name and Residence of Each Partner
  7. Contracts and Agreements
  8. Capital Contributions/Additional Contributions
  9. Allocation of Profits and Losses; Tax Credits and Deductions
 10. Book, Records, Bank Accounts, Checking
 11. Management and Responsibilities of the Parties
 12. Credits
 13. Warranties, Indemnification
 14. Exclusivity
 15. Dissolution and Termination of the Venture
 16. Distributions
 17. Gain or Loss During Dissolution
 18. Opportunities and Conflicts of Interest
 19. Death, Incapacity, Disability of a Partner
 20. Miscellaneous

(a) Notices	(f) Amendments
(b) Arbitration	(g) Additional Documents
(c) Applicable State Law	(h) Cumulative Remedies
(d) Law of Union Conflicts	(i) Written Consents
(e) Waiver	(j) Entire Agreement

Signatures

Advantages

Not securities. Interests in a joint venture are generally not considered securities; thus, it is not necessary to provide investors with a detailed securities disclosure document or otherwise comply with the burdensome federal and state securities laws.

Less documentation. A joint venture can be created with a joint venture agreement that is shorter and less complicated than the documentation associated with investment contracts, corporations or limited partnerships (i.e., securities documentation).

No formation filing. There is no required filing of a joint venture agreement with a secretary of state as is required for the limited partnership and corporate forms of doing business.

Corporate joint venturers. If both joint venture partners are corporations, the risks relating to the lack of limited liability for joint venture partners can be reduced.

Disadvantages

Limited term. The joint venture is not suitable for an ongoing long-term business.

Active partners. Each of the joint venture partners needs to be actively involved in the project.

Creative control. Since joint venturers will both (or all) be actively involved in the project, there may be disputes over creative issues.

Limited liability. The joint venture itself does not offer its joint-venture partner investors limited liability.

Tax withholdings. The joint venture is an entity separate from its joint venture partners and may be liable for tax withholdings on behalf of the joint venture.

Other tax consequences. Other unfavorable tax consequences may occur as a result of the creation of the joint venture entity.

Further Reading

Entertainment Industry Contracts: Motion Pictures. Vol. 1. Donald C. Farber. Matthew Bender, 1991.

Film Finance and Distribution—A Dictionary of Terms. John W. Cones. Silman-James Press, 1992.

Film Industry Contracts. John W. Cones. Self-published, 1993.

"Financing Film and Television Productions—Global Opportunities Emerging in the 1990's." Bruce St. J Lilliston. *Los Angeles Lawyer*, April 1990.

Joint Ventures: Structuring Alternatives. Shepard's, McGraw-Hill (updated periodically).

"JVC Goes Hollywood via Largo—Joint Venture with Gordon Marks Japan's U.S. Major Prod'n Debut with $100 Mil." Will Tusher. *Daily Variety*, August 21, 1989.

The Partnership Book: How to Write Your Own Small Business Partnership Agreement. Denis Clifford and Ralph Warner. Nolo Press, 1988.

The Small Business Form Book. Katherine L. Delsack. LawPrep Press, 1990.

18

The Initial Incorporation

An unincorporated production company that has been seeking funding for any number of purposes (e.g., development monies or production money for a single film or a slate of pictures) and that has engaged in a properly conducted general solicitation through the use of a business plan but has failed to identify that single active investor capable of funding the entire project through the investor-financing agreement (discussed above) may instead opt for the formation of a corporate production company. Assuming that the initial active investor general solicitation by means of the business plan resulted in interest from several prospective investors, none of whom are willing to fund the entire project but who are willing to join with the producer as founding shareholders of a newly organized corporation, then the producer may be in a position to execute the *initial incorporation* scenario without, technically, conducting a securities offering.

Although, technically speaking, corporate shares are securities and corporate shareholders are passive investors, thus generally requiring that the federal and state securities laws apply to the sale of corporate stock, a presumption may arise during the formation of a corporation that all of the founding shareholders are adequately informed regarding the corporation and/or have adequate means to protect their interests in the creation and operation of such entity. After all, the founding shareholders have an opportunity to get together in their first annual meeting and select the corporation's initial board of directors and some of the founding shareholders will likely be on the corporation's board, thus maintaining considerable control over the activities of the corporation. This in turn means that the shareholder/directors are no longer strictly passive investors, and they thus do not need the protection ordinarily provided by the securities laws that apply in the sale of corporate stock to outside shareholder prospects after a corporation has already been formed. That sort of secondary offering would surely require compliance with all of the federal and state securities laws that apply to any securities offering including the provision of a complete disclosure document to each prospective investor.

Forming a new corporation with a group of investors who are willing to be involved in the management of the corporation as shareholders, directors and/or officers allows the producer to avoid the time and expense involved in conducting a full-fledged securities offering (whether public or private). Such an offering would clearly be required if the producer first incorporated and then sought to raise money from a new, second group of shareholder/investors. On the other hand, the producer considering this strategy should obtain the advice of local counsel and/or discuss the issue with the state securities regulatory authority in the state in which the corporation is to be created to determine whether such an incorporation would require other necessary compliance with the state's securities laws (e.g., creation and use of a disclosure document). Some states may require that these initial shareholders have a certain level of sophistication with respect to the film industry before they can be appropriately characterized as active investors.

This strategy can work when the producer initially goes out into the marketplace to conduct a general solicitation by means of a generic business plan with the bona fide intent to find a single active investor or an active joint venture partner. Then, after failing to find such an active investor, the producer shifts his or her attention to the possibility of forming a corporation with several investors identified during the original general solicitation. In other words, the business plan must not precommit the producer to the initial incorporation strategy or the sale of any other security. If such language appears in the business plan, the general solicitation would have been conducted for the purpose of finding corporate shareholders who are ordinarily passive investors, and a general solicitation conducted for such prospective investors can only be done so legitimately following the registration of the securities with the Securities and Exchange Commission (SEC) at the federal level and with the state securities regulatory authorities in each state in which such sales or offers are contemplated or, in the alternative, by qualifying for available federal and state exemptions from such registration requirements (i.e., private placements).

Advantages

Avoids securities offering. If properly handled, this so-called initial incorporation technique can save the time, effort and money involved in the preparation of a complicated securities disclosure document and the conduct of a securities offering.

General corporate finance. As shareholders of the corporation, the initial investors are in a position to benefit from all of the corporation's activities to the extent that such activities are profitable and the board of directors chooses to declare dividends for the shareholders. The producer may also use this form of finance as an initial start-up phase, that is, raise a small amount of funds from a limited number of founding shareholders to cover film project acquisition, development and general corporate expenses, while relying on other forms of finance for the film's production costs.

Disadvantages

Some uncertainty. Such a strategy would probably not work with a large number of investors, and how many investors are too many cannot be predicted with certainty. Also, there is a need to determine whether any level of sophistication about the industry is required of these initial corporate shareholders.

Limited funds. The initial incorporation strategy is also only appropriate for raising a small amount of money for development and general corporate purposes from a limited number of founding shareholders, but again there are no official guides with regard to how much is too much or how many investors are too many.

Less control. In using this technique, the producer will, of necessity, have to give up some of his or her control of the company.

Further Reading

California Corporate Practice Guide. Morgan D. King. Lawpress Corporation, 1989.

California Corporation: How to Form Your Own. Anthony Mancuso. Nolo Press, 1988.

California Corporations Code and Corporate Securities Rules—1992 Edition. Matthew Bender, 1991.

California Corporation Start-Up Package and Minute Book. Kevin W. Finck. Oasis Press, 1987.

Choosing the Corporate Entity—S Corporations and Other Options After

Tax Reform. Gary A. Herrmann, Mark R. Ostler, and Michael S. Powlen. California Continuing Education of the Bar, Regents of the University of California, 1987.

"Commissions to Non-Broker/Dealers Under California Law." Elena R. Freshman. *Beverly Hills Bar Journal* 22, no. 2 (1988).

Film Finance and Distribution—A Dictionary of Terms. John W. Cones. Silman-James Press, 1992.

Film Industry Contracts. John W. Cones. Self-published, 1993.

Introduction to California Corporate Securities Practice. Norman A. Zilber, Ronald C. Carruth, Steven R. Dantzker, and Stephen M. Tennis. California Continuing Education of the Bar, Regents of the University of California, 1988.

Organizing and Advising Closely Held Corporations. State Bar of California, Continuing Education of the Bar seminar handbook, 1992.

Securities: Public and Private Offerings. William M. Prifti. Callaghan, 1983.

"Stocking It to 'Em—An Unusual Guarantee Prompts a Record Year for Initial Public Offerings." *California Lawyer,* March 1993.

"Wall Street on the Pacific—Investment Gurus Multiply in Hollywood's Backyard," Robert Marich and Jeffrey Daniels. *The Hollywood Reporter* (Entertainment Finance Special Report), January 29, 1993.

"Wall St. Puts Stock in IPOs—Entertainment Companies Brave Public Waters." Paul Noglows. *Variety,* p. 311, May 4, 1992.

"Where the Money Is." *The Hollywood Reporter* (Entertainment Finance Special Report), January 29, 1993.

19

The Investment Contract

An investment contract is a contractual arrangement through which a small group of passive investors provide financing for a project. It is more formally defined as a common enterprise involving an investment of funds by an investor or group of investors who hope to make a profit primarily based on the efforts of others, that is, the managers of the project. Since the investors are passive, the investment contract is a form of security; thus, the federal and state securities laws must be complied with when utilizing the investment contract to finance a film's development or production costs.

No limited liability. Since no entity has been created (e.g., limited partnership or corporation), this financing vehicle does not provide limited liability for the investors. However, some level of investor liability protection may be provided through indemnification and/or insurance.

Dollar amount. Because of the lack of limited liability, it is not practical to use the investment contract to raise large amounts of money. It is more appropriate for the investment contract to be used for ultralow budget film productions or for acquisition/development monies.

Disclosure issues. From a disclosure standpoint, and assuming the investment contract is to be used to raise small amounts of money (e.g., less than $500,000) in a private placement context, the producer/manager of the project will at a minimum be obligated to meet the requirements of the antifraud rule; that is, he or she must disclose in writing to each prospective investor all material aspects of the transaction. Some states may impose specific disclosure obligations on such offerings. In actual practice, it may be safer to rely on the specific disclosure guidelines of Regulation D, Rule 505, as opposed to making numerous judgment calls relating to individual disclosure questions that come up during the process of drafting the investment contract and/or an associated disclosure document.

Development money investment agreement. In situations where the investment contract is being used to raise money from passive investors for the development of a motion picture screenplay, it may be referred to as a Development Money Investment Agreement. On the other hand, if such funds are being raised from a single active investor, the transaction will probably not involve the securities laws. That agreement may still be called a Development Money Investment Agreement or in the alternative may be referred to as an Investor-Financing Agreement.

Investor-financing agreement. The investor-financing agreement is a contractual arrangement whereby a single active investor may invest funds to finance either the development or production costs of a motion picture project. The critical distinction is that with respect to the investor-financing agreement (as opposed to the investment contract) the investor must be actively involved in the management of the project on a regular basis in order to avoid the application of the securities laws.

Advantages

Less expensive. The investment contract offering is generally less expensive to mount than a limited partnership or corporate stock offering, thus may be more suitable for financing ultralow budget pictures or for raising acquisition and development moneys for a project.

No entity. The investment contract is merely a contractual arrangement. Therefore, it is not necessary to create and maintain an entity like the corporation or even a limited partnership.

Disadvantages

No limited liability. Unlike the limited partnership and corporation, the investment contract is not an entity and therefore does not provide limited liability to its investors. Thus, it is very important for the producer sponsor of an investment contract to obtain insurance coverages that will protect his or her investors from possible liability and to indemnify such investors where possible.

Not commonly known. Investors, accountants and even attorneys are generally not familiar with the use of an investment contract as a financing vehicle; thus, many of them will shy away from its use.

Further Reading

Film Finance and Distribution—A Dictionary of Terms. John W. Cones. Silman-James Press, 1992.

Film Industry Contracts. John W. Cones. Self-published, 1993.

"To Register or Not to Register—Is Broker/Dealer Registration for You?" James W. Ryan and Robert C. Beasley. *Texas Bar Journal*, June 1992.

20

Limited Partnerships

Formation and filings. All limited partnerships must have at least one general partner and one or more limited partners. The partners (both general and limited) must enter into a limited partnership agreement that should be in writing. However, no government review and approval is required for the limited partnership agreement associated with a privately placed limited partnership offering. A certificate of limited partnership signed by all of the general partners has to be filed with the secretary of state of the state in which the limited partnership is being formed. The filing of the certificate of limited partnership and thus the formation of the entity can wait until the offering is funded.

Name. The name of a limited partnership cannot be the same or similar to other limited partnerships already organized in that same state. A particular name can be reserved with or cleared by the secretary of state in some states, and the name is protected in the state by the filing of the limited partnership certificate. Further steps, however, may need to be taken in order to protect the name of the limited partnership outside the state of its formation. The names of limited partnerships generally are required to include the words *limited partnership* or the letters *L.P.* or *Ltd.* as part of the limited partnership's official name.

Cost of formation. The drafting of the partnership agreement itself is usually included in the cost of attorney preparation of the associated securities disclosure document. A filing fee in the $50 to $100 range is usually required to be paid to the secretary of state upon the formation of the limited partnership. Keep in mind that there is much more involved in a feature film limited partnership offering than merely creating the limited partnership entity.

Capital. Partners' capital contributions and loans to the partnership from partners and outsiders are typically the main sources of capital for the limited partnership. Quite often, most, if not all, of the capital contributions in the form of cash come from the limited partner investors.

Management and control. Management and control of the limited partnership is in the hands of the general partners. General partners may be individuals or corporations (or certain other entities). Limited partners may lose their limited liability if they participate in the control or management of the limited partnership (except for specific acts listed in the state statutes).

Liability of owners. General partners have unlimited liability to outsiders. Limited partners risk only the loss of their capital contribution unless they take part in management. Limited partners ordinarily are not required to guarantee partnership indebtedness.

Operations. Important transactions effected by the general partners do not require advance approval if such activities are in compliance with the partnership agreement and applicable state statutes. Significant corporate actions, on the other hand, require the support of board resolutions.

Books and records. The limited partnership is required to maintain certain books and records at its principal office, but the limited partnership books and records requirements are somewhat less burdensome than those for the corporation.

Sharing of profits. Limited partnerships provide considerably more flexibility in the structuring of profit-sharing arrangements between the general partner group and the limited partner investors pursuant to the partnership agreement.

Continuity of business. The limited partnership exists for a limited and stated term. Thus, it may be more suitable for project financing (i.e., one film or just a few films) as opposed to the long-term financing generally associated with general corporate finance. Dissolution of the limited partnership may result from the loss of a general partner but not from the loss of limited partners.

Transfer of interests. Restrictions on the transfer of limited partnership interests are imposed by state statute, the limited partnership agreement and/or the securities and tax laws. The general partner's right to receive distributions is typically assignable, but a transferee cannot be substituted as a general partner except by consent of the remaining partners (including the limited partners). Limited partners' interests are also assignable, but an assignee cannot be substituted as a limited partner without the other partners' consent, unless the partnership agreement provides otherwise. Substitution occurs when the limited partnership certificate is appropriately amended.

Fringe benefits. Some, but not all, of the fringe benefits that corporations can offer employees are now available to limited partnerships as well.

Taxation. Limited partnerships do not pay federal or state income tax (unless qualified as a publicly trading partnership under federal tax laws) but must file information returns. Both general and limited partners are taxed by the IRS on their share of the profits, whether distributed or not. The traditional double taxation of the corporate form is avoided through use of the limited partnership entity. Use of the limited partnership form may result in lower taxes generally, even without considering double taxation. If the partnership is the producing entity and it does not make enough money to return to the limited partners their total investment, the loss for income tax purposes is considered an ordinary loss, which may be offset against ordinary income. Most investors need a loss that can be offset against income more than they need a capital loss even though such passive activity losses can only be offset against passive activity gains. Limited partnerships doing business in a state such as California are subject to a franchise tax, but it is not prepaid as with corporations.

Owner identity. Limited partners' names often need not be disclosed to the public (depending on the state of formation); however, the name of the general partners are filed with the secretary of state.

Securities considerations. Interests in limited partnerships are securities and must be registered with federal and state authorities unless qualified for exemptions from registration (see discussions herein relating to various forms of "Private Placements").

Offering costs. Attorney fees for the lawyer's work involved in the preparation of a private placement feature film limited partnership offering disclosure document (offering memorandum) and related consultations regarding the proper conduct of the offering vary widely in terms of (1) an hourly or a flat fee, (2) how much is required up front, (3) fee deferrals, (4) whether the deferred portion is contingent on the success of the offering and (5) the specific tasks undertaken by the attorney. The typical flat fees may range from $10,000 to $50,000, depending on the experience and ability of the attorney. The attorney's fees associated with a public offering are generally higher. Also, the costs associated with the printing and binding of the disclosure documents and artwork, if any, must be considered. (The printing and binding costs for publicly offered disclosure documents are considerably more expensive because of the smaller unit size typical of the public offering—thus, more investors and more disclosure documents are needed). Accounting fees may be incurred for preparation of financial statements and/or projections. If used, broker/dealer due diligence expenses and commissions are limited by the rules of the National Association of Securities Dealers (NASD) to 10.5 percent of the offering proceeds in public offerings, but such commissions and fees are more flexible in the context of a private placement. Issuer marketing costs, which may be substantial, also might include phone, Federal Express, fax, postage, travel, finder's fees and the like.

Other states. If the limited partnership is actually doing business in a state other than the state of its formation, the laws of that other state regarding limited liability, foreign limited partnerships and so forth must be considered.

Advantages

More flexibility. The limited partnership offers more flexibility in structuring the deal between management and the investors compared with corporations.

Lower maintenance. The limited partnership is generally less cumbersome to maintain than a corporation. Fewer meetings are required.

Single picture financing. The limited partnership may be more suitable for single picture financing because it is a limited term entity.

Flow-through tax vehicle. The limited partnership still has one significant tax benefit over the regular C corporation, that is, the limited partnership entity itself is not taxed at the entity level. Revenues to the partnership flow through to the partners and are only taxed at the individual level.

Disadvantages

Sour market. The many thousands of investors who put money into the large public film limited partnerships of the eighties experienced disappointing financial results and are not likely to be interested in any sort of similar offering unless it is clearly distinguished from the earlier offerings in a persuasive manner.

Securities law compliance. Compliance with the dual system of securities law regulation (both federal and state) can be overly burdensome for small production companies.

Fewer significant tax advantages. There are not as many significant tax advantages that favor the use of the limited partnership as an investment vehicle in the United States as there were before the 1986 Tax Reform Act.

Securities attorney. Because of the complexity of the federal and state securities laws, it may be necessary to retain the services and pay the fees of an experienced securities attorney, specifically a securities attorney with feature-film limited partnership experience.

Further Reading

"Cable Investors on Roll, Study Says." David Kelly. *The Hollywood Reporter,* July 12, 1991.

"Commissions to Non-Broker/Dealers Under California Law." Elena R. Freshman. *Beverly Hills Bar Journal* 22, no. 2 (1988).

"Feature Film Limited Partnerships: A Practical Guide Focusing on Securities and Marketing for Independent Producers and Their Attorneys." John W. Cones. *Loyola of Los Angeles Entertainment Law Journal* 12, no. 1 (1992).

Federal Taxation of Partnerships and Partners. 2d ed. William S. McKee, William F. Nelson, and Robert L. Whitmire. Warren Gorham and Lamont (updated periodically).

Film Finance and Distribution—A Dictionary of Terms. John W. Cones. Silman-James Press, 1992.

Film Industry Contracts. John W. Cones. Self-published, 1993.

"Financial Guidelines for Investing in Motion Picture Limited Partnerships." L. M. Farrell. *Loyola of Los Angeles Entertainment Law Journal* 12, no. 1 (1992).

"Financing the Production of Theatrical Motion Pictures." Lionel S. Sobel. *Entertainment Law Reporter,* May 1984.

"The Indies are Glowing But Capital Not Flowing." Christian Moerk. *Variety* (Entertainment Finance Special Report), March 22, 1993.

"U.S. Filmers Find Angels Overseas—Indies, in a Conservative Mode, Gather Coin from Afar and Tighten Their Belts." Christian Moerk. *Variety,* October 12, 1992.

What a Producer Does. Buck Houghton. American Film Institute, 1991.

21

Limited Liability Companies

The limited liability company (LLC) is a relatively new form of business entity now available in almost every state. The LLC combines aspects of the corporation and the limited partnership. It has managers who correspond to the corporation's board of directors and officers and the limited partnership's general partner. It also has members who own interests in the company. The members correspond to the corporate shareholders and the limited partnership's limited partner investors. Both managers and members enjoy limited liability.

The LLC may be operated either in the fairly democratic tradition of a general partnership or in the more centralized manner of a corporation with a board of directors and officers. In the first instance, interests in an active-investor LLC may not be considered a security. Thus, it may be characterized as an active-investor vehicle. It is important, however, to obtain assurances from the state regulatory authority in the state in which the LLC is being created regarding the limited circumstances under which an interest in an LLC may be treated as non-security. Otherwise, the LLC should be treated as a passive-investor vehicle and, thus, a security.

In any case, the LLC is a flexible form of doing business that provides its member/investors with corporate-type limited liability, while still allowing the benefits of partnership ("flow through") tax status. It may engage in any lawful business or purpose including the production and distribution of a feature film.

The limited liability company is formed much like a corporation in that one or more of the company's organizers must file articles of organization (as opposed to the corporate articles of incorporation) with the secretary of state in the state in which the company is being organized. In addition, the company may (but does not have to) adopt regulations that are somewhat analogous to a corporation's bylaws or the limited partnership's limited partnership agreement. These are typically referred to as the LLC operating agreement and commonly appear as Exhibit "A" to the LLC disclosure document.

For federal income tax purposes, the limited liability company is treated much like the S corporation or the limited partnership; that is, the company is not taxed at the entity level. However, unlike the limited partnership, whose individual general partners do not have limited liability, the individual managers of the LLC (and the LLC's members) all can enjoy limited liability. Thus, the LLC may be of particular interest to low budget independent filmmakers who do not want to create and maintain a second entity (a corporation) for purposes of gaining limited liability for the management of the investment vehicle.

Unlike an S corporation, the limited liability company can have subsidiaries and can allocate benefits differently among its owners (the S corporation can only have one class of stock).

Advantages

Best of both worlds. The limited liability company combines the tax benefits of a partnership with the limited liability benefits provided by a corporation.

Flexibility. Limited liability companies are generally more flexible with regard to certain issues than either S corporations or limited partnerships.

Informal and democratic operations. The company can be operated in a fairly democratic and informal manner like a general partnership (an active investor/non-securities investment vehicle) without the burdens of the more formal corporate maintenance.

Disadvantages

Corporate franchise tax. In most states the limited liability company is subject to the corporate franchise tax just like a corporation.

Not recognized in all states. This new form of doing business may not be recognized in all states; thus, its usefulness may be limited to the states that have adopted limited liability company legislation. On the other hand, most states have now adopted the LLC form of doing business.

Piercing the limited liability veil. Like corporations, it may be possible for creditors and others to pierce the shell of limited liability and make the managers and members personally liable. There is little case law available to give attorneys and others guidance on that issue, except law associated with corporations and limited partnerships, which may be used by analogy.

Not for many owners. The limited liability company is not very useful for business entities involving a large number of owners because of restrictions that may require the company's dissolution upon the death, dissolution or bankruptcy of a member.

Member Voting Rights. Some states also require that the LLC's member/investors be permitted to vote on important issues and allow a simple majority to control the decision.

Further Reading

"Business Law Update—The Texas Limited Liability Company and the Registered Limited Liability Partnership." Edgardo E. Colon. *Texas Bar Journal*, October 1993: 908.

Film Finance and Distribution—A Dictionary of Terms. John W. Cones. Silman-James Press, 1992.

How to Form and Operate a Limited Liability Company. Gregory C. Damman, J.D. Self-Counsel Press, Inc., 1995.

"Limited Liability Companies—New Possibilities for Texas Business Organization." Eddy J. Rogers, Jr., and Blakely Rogers Stinebaugh. *Texas Bar Journal*, July 1992.

"LLCs Offer Alternatives to Industry." Robert L. Siegel. *Entertainment Law & Finance*, January 1995.

"LLC's Offer New Hybrid Business Structure." Heltsley. *Arizona Daily Star*, October 15, 1992.

"A Practical Primer on the Business Laws and Tax Aspects of Using a Limited Liability Company." William K. Norman. *Beverly Hills Bar Journal*, Spring 1993.

Taxation of Limited Liability Companies. David J. Cartano. http://www.loop.com/~cartano/llc.htm. 1996.

"Trading Angels and Blue Skies for Straight Capitalism." Michael Barnes and Kevin Morris. *Filmmaker*, Spring 1993.

22

Corporate Financing

A corporation is a statutory entity created and regulated by state laws. A corporation has its own legal identity separate from any of the people who own, control, manage or operate it. It is a legal person capable of entering into contracts, incurring debts and paying taxes. Thus, the corporation is a separate taxable entity. The corporation is created by taking the following steps: (1) drafting and filing articles of incorporation with the secretary of state of the state in which the corporation is being created; (2) obtaining the secretary of state's approval of the articles; (3) obtaining a certificate of incorporation from the secretary of state; (4) conducting an initial meeting of shareholders of the corporation and naming a board of directors; and (5) conducting an initial meeting of the board of directors and naming officers, setting up a bank account, approving the corporate seal, approving corporate bylaws and issuing shares.

In some states—California, for example—a notice of sale regarding the issuance of the corporation's initial shares must be filed with the Department of Corporations, and a Statement of Domestic Corporation must be filed within ninety days. Generally, the corporation is formed first, and then an offering of shares is conducted to those beyond the initial founding shareholders in public or private offerings (see chapter 18).

The corporation's name cannot be the same or similar to other corporations in that same state; thus, the name must be reserved with or cleared by the secretary of state. The name is protected by filing the corporation's articles but may need to be protected outside the state with trademark registration or "doing business" filings in each state.

A filing fee is generally required when filing the articles of incorporation. In California, for example, the filing fee is $70. Other state filing fees may differ. Also, a minimum franchise tax prepaid deposit may be required (California is on the high end). Corporate kits should also be purchased. The kits typically include sample bylaws, sample minutes, a corporate seal, share certificates and a stock transfer log, and they cost from $50 to $100. Attorney fees for a simple incorporation may start at $1,000 or so.

Capital. The sale of corporate shares (equity ownership interests) may be made in various forms, including common, preferred, and convertible stocks. Also, corporate debt instruments can be issued in various forms, including bonds, debentures, notes and other evidences of indebtedness.

Management and control. Corporate management and control is highly centralized in officers and directors. Many control devices are available to separate management from ownership, such as nonvoting stock, voting trusts, shareholder agreements and super majority vote requirements for certain matters.

Owner identity. Shareholder identities are not disclosed on public records in most states, but the names of the corporation's officers and directors are filed and are thus available through inspection of the public records.

Offering costs. Just as with a limited partnership offering, attorney fees for private offerings of corporate stock vary widely in terms of *(a)* an hourly or a flat fee *(b)* how much is required up front, *(c)* whether some of the fee may be deferred and *(d)* whether the deferred portion is contingent on the success of the offering. Attorney fees may range from $10,000 to $50,000, depending on the attorney or law firm and what services are included. An attorney or law firm will generally charge more for a public offering of corporate stock. The costs for printing, artwork and binding for the disclosure document (*prospectus* for public offerings and *offering memorandum* for private placements) also must be considered. The printing cost for the public offering prospectus is typically much greater than for a private offering because of the smaller unit size of the public offering and the need for a significantly larger number of disclosure documents. Accounting fees may be incurred in the preparation of financial statements and/or projections that may be included in the disclosure document as exhibits. Also, if broker/dealers are used to raise funds, they may require up-front due diligence fees and the reimbursement of due diligence expenses. Broker/dealer commissions and expenses are limited in public offerings by the rules of the NASD (10.5% ceiling for public offerings, but more flexible for private offerings). Issuer marketing costs also may be substantial.

Advantages

Long-term ventures. The corporate structure is most suitable for a long-term ongoing business as opposed to project financing of a single feature film or limited number of movies. Corporations generally are created to have perpetual existence but may be dissolved.

Doing business with others. Many other businesses, for example, banks, prefer to do business with corporations in some circumstances.

Liability of owners. Risks are primarily borne by the corporation. Shareholders risk only their investment, not their personal estates, unless there are defects in the organization or the corporation has been improperly maintained. Officers and directors may incur liability for certain acts or omissions. Lenders may require personal guarantees of principal shareholders of closely held corporations.

Transfer of ownership. Corporate shares may be more readily transferable than interests in partnerships if there is a market for them. However, restrictions on sale to outsiders may be imposed by the corporation's articles, its bylaws, shareholder agreements or federal and state securities laws.

Tax considerations. Business income can be sheltered in the corporation and reported and taxed at the business (corporate) level only.

Favored tax benefits. The corporation is eligible for tax deductible employee fringe benefits paid to its employees. Many tax-favored fringe benefits are available for corporate employees, such as profit-sharing and pension plans, group insurance, and accident, health and sick-pay plans.

S corporation alternative. Use of an S corporation may reduce the federal tax burden on the corporation (see chapter 24).

Disadvantages

Securities considerations. Debt and equity interests in corporations are securities and must be registered with federal and state authorities unless qualified for exemptions from registration (private placements).

Taxation. Corporations are taxed by the Internal Revenue Service on pre-dividend profits, and shareholders are taxed on dividends, if any, which may result in the double taxation of the same revenue stream, once at the corporate level and again at the shareholder level. If the corporation is the producing entity of a feature film and it loses money, the loss is in the nature of a capital loss. Most investors need a loss that can offset income more than they need a capital loss (see chapter 20).

Franchise tax. An annual state franchise tax is imposed on corporations in most states and must be prepaid upon formation.

Operations. Many corporate officer actions require resolutions approved by the corporation's board of directors in addition to compliance with any applicable statutes, the corporation's articles of incorporation and its bylaws.

Foreign corporations. A corporation doing business in another state may have to register as a foreign corporation and pay taxes in that state on the portion of its revenues derived from doing business in that state.

Books and records. The corporation is required to follow specific formalities including the creation and maintenance of its initial organizational minutes, shareholder meeting minutes and minutes of board of directors' meetings. The corporation must elect directors, adopt bylaws, issue shares, record transfers, conduct annual shareholder meetings, keep minutes of the board's actions, prepare and publish annual financial statements, provide reports to shareholders and submit periodic SEC filings under some circumstances.

Sharing of profits. Corporate profits are paid to shareholders by means of corporate dividends in exact proportion to the ownership interests of the shareholders and at the discretion of the corporation's board of directors.

Suspension of powers. A corporation's powers may be suspended for failure to comply with certain of the corporate formalities described above.

Further Reading

California Corporate Practice Guide. Morgan D. King. Lawpress Corporation, 1989.

California Corporation—How to Form Your Own. Anthony Mancuso. Nolo Press, 1988.

California Corporations Code and Corporate Securities Rules—1992 Edition. Matthew Bender, 1991.

California Corporation Start-Up Package and Minute Book. Kevin W. Finck. Oasis Press, 1987.

Choosing the Corporate Entity—S Corporations and Other Options after Tax Reform. Gary A. Herrmann, Mark R. Ostler, and Michael S.

Powlen. California Continuing Education of the Bar, Regents of the University of California, 1987.

"Commissions to Non-Broker/Dealers Under California Law." Elena R. Freshman. *Beverly Hills Bar Journal* 22, no. 2 (1988).

Film Finance and Distribution—A Dictionary of Terms. John W. Cones. Silman-James Press, 1992.

Film Industry Contracts. John W. Cones. Self-published, 1993.

Introduction to California Corporate Securities Practice. Norman A. Zilber, Ronald C. Carruth, Steven R. Dantzker, and Stephen M. Tennis. California Continuing Education of the Bar, Regents of the University of California, 1988.

Organizing and Advising Closely Held Corporations. State Bar of California, Continuing Education of the Bar seminar handbook, 1992.

Securities: Public and Private Offerings. William M. Prifti. Callaghan, 1983.

"Stocking It To 'Em"—An Unusual Guarantee Prompts a Record Year for Initial Public Offerings. *California Lawyer*, March 1993.

"Wall Street on the Pacific—Investment Gurus Multiply in Hollywood's Backyard." Robert Marich and Jeffrey Daniels. *The Hollywood Reporter* (Entertainment Finance Special Report), January 29, 1993.

"Wall St. Puts Stock in IPOs—Entertainment Companies Brave Public Waters." Paul Noglows. *Variety*, p. 311, May 4, 1992.

"Where the Money Is." *The Hollywood Reporter* (Entertainment Finance Special Report), January 29, 1993.

23

The Out-of-State Corporation

The following points relate specifically to the question of whether to incorporate as an out-of-state corporation and do business in California, but the reasoning may apply by analogy to some extent to other states. Feature film producers are advised to consult with an attorney or accountant (or both) before making this decision.

Qualification. All out-of-state corporations (also referred to as foreign corporations) transacting business within California must qualify with the California secretary of state. To become qualified, a foreign corporation must first apply for registration with the secretary of state. The application for registration must be accompanied by a Certificate of Good Standing executed by an authorized public official of the state or place in which the corporation is organized. A qualification fee must also accompany the application.

Annual report. After a foreign corporation is qualified to do business in a state, in addition to the reporting requirements of the corporation's state of organization, an annual report may be required to be filed with that state's secretary of state. A corporation can forfeit its powers or rights by failing to file its annual statement.

Franchise tax. An annual franchise tax based on the amount of net profits earned in California must be paid to California.

Application of corporation code provisions. A foreign corporation that does more than half of its business in California and has half of its shareholders in California is subject to many of the same provisions of the California Corporations Code that apply to domestic corporations.

Forfeiture. If a foreign corporation fails to properly qualify itself, the exercise of its corporate powers, rights and privileges in California may be forfeited. If forfeited, all contracts made by a non-qualified foreign corporation are voidable at the option of the other party. Forfeiture usually takes effect upon the Franchise Tax Board's transmission of the name of the delinquent corporate taxpayer to the secretary of state. The secretary of state may also forfeit the right of a foreign corporation to transact intrastate business in California on its own volition.

Other penalties. A foreign corporation's failure to qualify or be in good standing to transact intrastate business in California may result in its inability to maintain any cause of action in a California court. A fine for pursuing such a suit may be imposed. A foreign corporation that transacts intrastate business without holding a valid Certificate of Registration may also be subject to a daily penalty for each day unauthorized business is transacted. Such a corporation may also be held guilty of a misdemeanor, punishable by a fine.

Summary. Based on the above, it may be safe to conclude that the supposed benefits to most small corporations of incorporating out of state are outweighed by the costs and burdens of qualifying to do business in California as a foreign corporation.

Advantages

Avoidance of California state taxation. This is the single most popular reason put forth by film producers trying to decide whether to incorporate their production companies as a California corporation.

Local production company. An independent producer who actually operates out of another state and seeks to raise funds from investors in that state for a local film production may find it advantageous to organize as a local corporation.

Disadvantages

Tax liabilities not entirely avoided. As discussed above, incorporating out of state does not always avoid the imposition of taxes on income generated by out-of-state corporations actually doing business in California.

Second level of bureaucracy. If in fact the production company is organized as an out-of-state corporation but is actually doing business in California, it appears that the producer incorporating out of state has merely superimposed a second level of rules, paperwork and expense on the corporation's operations.

Further Reading

California Corporate Practice Guide 2d. Morgan D. King. Lawpress Corporation, 1989.

California Corporation Start-Up Package and Minute Book. Kevin W. Finck. Oasis Press, 1987.

Film Finance and Distribution—A Dictionary of Terms. John W. Cones. Silman-James Press, 1992.

Film Industry Contracts. John W. Cones. Self-published, 1993.

Understanding the Securities Laws. Larry D. Soderquist. Practicing Law Institute, 1990.

24

S Corporations

Once the decision has been made to finance a film or films using investor financing generally, as opposed to the various studio/ industry, lender or foreign financing alternatives, and the corporate vehicle is chosen specifically, the producer must still decide whether to opt for an S corporation or a regular C corporation. A corporation that satisfies the requirements of subchapter S (now referred to as an S corporation) is taxed differently than a regular C corporation (IRC Section 1362).

Basic Characteristics of an S Corporation

No federal entity level taxation. With the exception of certain capital gains, an S corporation bears no federal income tax consequences at the corporate level. However, the state of California imposes a 2.5 percent tax on the taxable income of an S corporation.

Shareholder taxation. The shareholders of an S corporation are taxed on all income of the corporation with a few exceptions, regardless of whether or not the income is actually distributed to the shareholders; that is, a cash distribution to investors is not a taxable event, but the receipt of income for accounting purposes is a taxable event (IRC Section 1366).

Requirements of an S Corporation

The failure to meet any of the requirements listed below will cause the disqualification of the entity as an S corporation effective on the date of the failure.

Timely election required. To be taxed as an S corporation, a timely election must be made by the corporation under IRC Section 1362. That election must be made for the current year on or before the fifteenth day of the third month of the taxable year (or prior to the first day of the year to come) in order to be effective for that year.

113

Calendar year. An S corporation must use a calendar year, unless it establishes a business purpose for a fiscal year.

Unanimous consent. All shareholders of the corporation and persons who have an interest in the stock must consent to the S corporation election.

Domestic corporations only. The corporation must be a U.S. domestic corporation and cannot be a member of an affiliated group of corporations, nor a financial institution or insurance company. An S corporation can own up to 25 percent of the stock in another corporation.

Limited number of shareholders. The maximum number of shareholders is limited to thirty-five (a husband and wife are treated as one shareholder as is the case of stock owned by a trust or other qualifying estate).

Only individual shareholders. A shareholder must be an individual (U.S. citizen or resident), an estate, or a Qualified Subchapter S Trust. Thus, no corporations or partnerships may be shareholders of an S corporation.

Only one class of stock. Only one class of stock may be issued and outstanding (although there may be differences as to the voting rights among stockholders; e.g., it is currently permissible to have voting and nonvoting common stock). Corporate debt may be allowed if it is not a disguised second class of stock. Proposed IRS regulations concerning the "one class of stock" requirement must be carefully considered when issuing stock other than ordinary common stock.

No foreign shareholders. A nonresident alien (foreigner) may not be a shareholder in an S corporation. Be especially careful with loans from foreigners, particularly if those loans have equity features.

Tax Features of Operating as an S Corporation

Pass-through vehicle. Income, losses, deductions and credits are passed through to shareholders on a per-share, per-day basis.

Shareholder basis. The shareholder basis is increased by income, contributions and loans to the corporation but decreased by losses and distributions.

Losses carried forward. Losses in excess of stock and debt basis are suspended and carried forward.

Tax-free distributions. If the corporation has no earnings and profits, distributions not in excess of basis are tax-free. Distributions in excess of basis are capital gains.

Taxation of dividends. Earnings and profits are taxable as dividends when distributed.

Corporate level taxation. There is a tax applied at the corporate level on certain long-term capital gains or built-in gains. There is also a corporate-level tax on excess passive income of a former C corporation that has earnings and profits.

Termination

The S corporation election will be terminated immediately if noneligible shareholders or too many shareholders acquire stock. The election will also be terminated immediately if the corporation ceases to be a small business corporation. Following termination, no new election can be made for five years. Relief may be available for inadvertent termination. The election will be terminated on the first day of the fourth year if the corporation has earnings and profits and excessive passive income for three consecutive years.

Summary

If earnings are not to be reinvested. An S corporation election is generally desirable when the business is expected to make a profit soon after incorporation and there will be little need to reinvest earnings in the business for expansion. In that case, the corporation will likely distribute most of its net income to shareholders, and so by making an S election, the double taxation of a regular C corporation would be avoided.

If earnings are to be reinvested. On the other hand, if profits are going to be reinvested in the business for a few years, then an S election is probably not desirable because there would be no double taxation anyway since earnings are being reinvested rather than distributed to shareholders.

Advantages

Flow-through vehicle. The S Corporation (generally speaking) is considered a *flow-through* vehicle for federal income tax purposes; that is, the entity itself is not subject to the payment of most federal income taxes.

Ordinary losses. Corporate operating losses are deductible as ordinary losses by the shareholders, pro rata, up to their basis in the stock.

Avoidance of double taxation. The double taxation normally associated with a regular corporation can be avoided by using the S corporation status.

Expected profits. The S corporation is a good idea if the corporation is expected to earn profits right away and there is no need to reinvest earnings in the corporation.

Family income. The S corporation election allows corporate income to be spread among various family members to minimize the total income tax for the family as a whole.

Disadvantages

Shareholder limit. The number of shareholders is limited to thirty-five.

Termination. The S corporation special status may be terminated if noneligible shareholders or too many shareholders acquire stock.

Nonresident aliens. Nonresident aliens may not be shareholders in S corporations.

Single class of stock. S corporations can only offer one class of stock.

Individual shareholders. Generally speaking, shareholders must be individuals.

Professional advice. The decision to choose this form of conducting business should almost certainly involve the professional advice of an accountant or tax attorney.

Effect of 1993 Act. Following passage of the Revenue Reconciliation Act of 1993, S corporations that retain earnings to fund growth may want to rethink their S corporation status if shareholders will be in higher tax brackets than the corporation would be if it terminated its S corporation election.

Further Reading

California Corporate Practice Guide 2d. Morgan D. King. Lawpress Corporation, 1989.

California Corporation Start-Up Package and Minute Book. Kevin W. Finck. Oasis Press, 1987.

Choosing the Corporate Entity: S Corporations and Other Options after Tax Reform. Gary A. Herrmann, Mark R. Ostler, and Michael S. Powlen. California Continuing Education of the Bar, Regents of the University of California, 1987.

Film Finance & Distribution—A Dictionary of Terms. John W. Cones. Silman-James Press, 1992.

How to Form Your Own California Corporation. Anthony Mancus. Nolo Press, 1988.

Revenue Reconciliation Act of 1993—Law and Explanation. Commerce Clearing House, August 1993.

Revenue Reconciliation Act of 1993—Professional Summary. Commerce Clearing House, August 1993.

S Corporations Guide. Edward C. Foth and Ted D. Engelbrecht. Commerce Clearing House (updated periodically).

"Trading Angels and Blue Skies for Straight Capitalism." Michael Barnes and Kevin Morris. *Filmmaker*, Spring 1993.

25

Small Corporate Offering Registration

This form of corporate securities registration (public offering) is designed to reduce the costs and paperwork involved in public offerings, thus diminishing the burden on small businesses that seek to raise capital. The North American Securities Administrators Association (NASAA), an association of state securities regulators, adopted the Small Corporate Offering Registration (SCOR) Form (U-7) on April 29, 1989, and many state legislatures around the country have since adopted state legislation patterned after the NASAA model. The Form U-7 was developed pursuant to Congress's Small Business Investment Incentive Act of 1980 (now contained in Section 19 of the federal Securities Act of 1933).

Form U-7 is the general public-offering registration form for corporations registering under state securities (blue-sky) laws that provide exemptions from the registration requirements of the federal Securities and Exchange Commission compatible with the SEC's Rule 504 of Regulation D.

To be eligible to use the Form U-7, a company (1) must be a corporation organized under the laws of the state in which the offering is to be filed and (2) must engage in a business other than petroleum exploration or production and mining or other extractive industries. Thus, feature film production companies qualify. *Blind pool* offerings and other offerings for which the specific business or properties cannot now be described are ineligible to use Form U-7. In other words, film producers cannot raise a fund for use in producing unspecified film properties using the Form U-7.

The company's securities may be offered and sold only on behalf of the company, and Form U-7 may not be used by any present security holders of the company who are trying to resell their securities. The offering price for common stock must be equal to or greater than five dollars per share. Also, the company must agree not to split its common stock or declare a stock dividend for two years after effectiveness of the registration without the permission of the state regulators involved.

Companies using the Form U-7 may engage selling agents to sell their securities. However, commissions, fees or other remuneration for soliciting any prospective purchaser may only be paid to persons who are registered as securities broker/dealers in the state in which sales occur. Thus, finders who by definition are not registered securities broker/dealers may not be paid so-called finder's fees.

Advantages

Disclosure document. The Form U-7 itself, once filled out, filed and declared effective, constitutes the offering circular or prospectus (disclosure document) for the offering and may be reproduced by the company by copy machine or otherwise for dissemination to prospective investors.

Attorney not necessarily needed. Some producers may be comfortable with their ability to complete the registration form and conduct the offering without the assistance of counsel so long as the state securities laws are also complied with (but see *Attorney's opinion* below).

Disadvantages

No sales until effective. No offers or sales may be made until the registration has been declared effective by the state regulator.

Selling materials must be approved. Any and all supplemental selling literature or advertisements announcing the offering must be filed by the company and cleared with the state securities regulator of each state prior to publication or circulation within that state.

Content of public announcements. The information contained in public announcements regarding the offering is specifically limited.

Disclosure requirements. The disclosures required by Form U-7 are very similar to those required in other securities offerings.

Ceiling on amount of money raised. The form can only be used if the total amount of money being raised does not exceed $1 million during a twelve-month period.

Form D required. A completed and signed SEC Form D must also be filed with the SEC, claiming exemption from the federal securities registration requirement (pursuant to Regulation D, Rule 504).

Attorney's opinion. An opinion of an attorney licensed to practice in the state of registration must be submitted to the state regulator. In that opinion, the attorney must state that the securities to be sold in the offering have been duly authorized and, when issued upon payment of the offering price, will be legally and validly issued, fully paid and nonassessable and binding on the company.

Further Reading

Film Finance and Distribution—A Dictionary of Terms. John W. Cones. Silman-James Press, 1992.

Small Corporate Offering Registration Form (U-7). North American Securities Administrators Association, April 29, 1989.

"To Register or Not to Register—Is Broker/Dealer Registration for You?" James W. Ryan and Robert C. Beasley. *Texas Bar Journal*, June 1992.

"Trading Angels and Blue Skies for Straight Capitalism." Michael Barnes and Kevin Morris. *Filmmaker*, Spring 1993.

26

Regulation A Offerings

Although the language of the SEC's Regulation A does not technically so state, Regulation A is actually a small public (registered) offering provision that permits the feature film producer (or other issuer of securities) to conduct some limited advertising. Regulation A limits the amount of money that can be raised during any given one-year period to $5 million, certainly enough for most low-budget feature film projects.

Prefiling. The regulation requires that at least ten days (Saturdays, Sundays and holidays excluded) prior to the date on which the initial offering or sale of the securities is to be made under the regulation, the producer must file with the SEC regional office five copies of the offering statement required by Regulation A. That offering statement consists of Part I—Notification, Part II—Offering Circular and Part III—Exhibits. Instead of an *offering circular* (the term used by Regulation A instead of *offering memorandum* or *prospectus* for the securities *disclosure document*), Regulation A also now permits the use of a fill-in-the-blank form similar to the SCOR Form U-7.

Disclosure document. No written offer of the securities can be made unless an offering circular (or completed form) containing the required disclosures (the information specified in Part II of the offering statement) is concurrently given or has previously been given to the person to whom the offer is made. Also, no securities of the issuer (production company) can be sold under Regulation A unless the offering circular or the completed fill-in-the-blank form is furnished to the prospective investor at least forty-eight hours prior to the mailing of the confirmation of sale by the production company (issuer) and the SEC has not disallowed the offering.

Advertising limits. Written advertisements or other written communications and radio or television broadcasts can contain no more than the following information:

121

- The name of the issuer of the security
- The title of the security, for example, corporate stock or limited partnership interest
- The amount being offered (the aggregate offering price or total amount of money being raised)
- The per-unit offering price to the public
- The identity of the general type of business of the issuer (for example, and development of feature films)
- A brief statement as to the general character of the film project
- From whom an offering circular can be obtained

Sales materials. Four copies of all of the sales materials prepared in conjunction with the Regulation A offering must also be submitted to the SEC.

Revised circular. If the offering is not completed within nine months from the date of the offering circular, a revised offering circular must be prepared, filed and used in accordance with the Regulation A rules.

Test-the-waters provision. Another recent change in the Regulation A procedures allows the feature film producer (securities issuer) to engage in a so-called testing of the waters, that is, to publicly disseminate an executive summary of the proposed offering in order to gather expressions of interest from prospective investors. The idea here is that it is much less expensive to disseminate a four- or five-page summary of the offering than the entire offering circular. A similar testing of the waters can be accomplished through the proper drafting and circulation of a generic business plan not specifically associated with a possible subsequent securities offering but instead tied to an investor-financing agreement, joint venture or initial incorporation possibility (see chapters 16–18).

State coordination. Unfortunately, many states have not yet adopted provisions compatible with the SEC's Regulation A test-the-waters provision, and since the securities laws require compliance with both the federal and state laws, the Regulation A test-the-waters provision may not be useful in those nonadopting states. Thus, the status of the applicable provisions in each state in which offers or sales are anticipated must be determined and complied with.

Reports of sales. Within thirty days after the end of each six-month period following the date of the original offering circular (or form), the producer must file with the SEC's regional office a completed SEC Form 2-A, and a final report must be submitted upon completion or termination of the offering but no later than six months from the last sale.

Advantages

Public offering. Regulation A is a form of small public offering; thus, the producer can conduct a general solicitation (including "cold calls" and mass mailings) and engage in some advertising to raise money.

Test the waters. The newly revised Regulation A allows producers to disseminate summaries of their planned offerings to gauge investor interest before incurring the expense of printing and binding hundreds of offering circulars or other forms of disclosure documents (also see chapter 15).

SEC filing. The required SEC filing may be effected through the nearest regional office of the SEC.

Disadvantages

Prefiling. A proper filing must be effected prior to any sales.

State law may differ. Regulation A is not fully coordinated with state law.

Dual regulation. Compliance with both federal and state rules is required.

Offering price ceiling. Although $5 million is enough to allow for the production of most low-budget feature films, this ceiling on the amount of money that can be raised pursuant to Regulation A does prevent higher-budget pictures from relying on Regulation A.

Further Reading

Blue Sky Laws—A Course Handbook. Jack H. Halperin and F. Lee Liebolt, Jr. Practicing Law Institute, 1990.

"Entertainment Finance 1990: Entering a Brave New World." Robert Marich. *The Hollywood Reporter* (Entertainment Finance Special Report), p. F-3, August 1990.

Film Finance and Distribution—A Dictionary of Terms. John W. Cones. Silman-James Press, 1992.

Film Industry Contracts. John W. Cones. Self-published, 1993.

"Pix Go Public—Indies Dance to 'Reg A.' " Andrew J. Neff. *Daily Variety*, June 5, 1979.

Regulation A—Under the Securities Act of 1933. Bowne, 1993.

"Trading Angels and Blue Skies for Straight Capitalism." Michael Barnes and Kevin Morris, *Filmmaker*, Spring 1993.

27

Regulation S-B Public Offerings

The SEC's Regulation S-B is another form of public (registered) securities offering for small business issuers including corporations and limited partnerships. For purposes of the regulation, the small business issuer is defined as a U.S. or Canadian company with revenues of less than $25 million (if the company is a majority-owned subsidiary, the parent corporation must also be a small business issuer).

Regulation S-B does require that the producer (issuer) provide a disclosure document (prospectus) to each prospective investor prior to the investment and the regulation sets out in fairly rigorous detail the kinds of information that must be included in the disclosure document. For example, the following information must be provided (this is not a complete list of Regulation S-B disclosure requirements):

- A description of the business of the issuer (including form and year of organization)
- A statement declaring whether the issuer is a party to any pending legal proceedings
- Certain financial statements of existing companies
- The issuer's directors, executive officers or upper-level management
- Management compensation in all forms
- Specific information that must appear on the outside front cover of the prospectus
- A summary of the prospectus (under some circumstances)
- A discussion of any factors that make the offering speculative or risky (risk factors)
- A statement regarding how the net proceeds of the offering will be used (use of proceeds)
- The issuer's plan for selling the securities (plan of distribution of the securities)
- Certain exhibits such as existing material contracts and attorney's opinions (under some circumstances)
- Other special disclosures relating specifically to the nature of the issuing entity, that is, whether corporation or limited partnership

Financial projections. Unlike earlier years, the SEC now encourages the use of management's projections of future economic performance in conjunction with public offerings like the Regulation S-B provisions. However, the SEC does require that such financial projections have a reasonable basis and that they be presented in an appropriate format (as set out in more detail in Regulation S-B).

Advantages

Advertising permitted. A public (registered) offering such as a Regulation S-B offering permits advertising to the general public and marketing techniques that fall under the label *general solicitation*.

Compared to Form S-1 offerings. A Regulation S-B offering is somewhat less burdensome than a Form S-1 securities offering (see chapter 28).

Key employees. A publicly held corporation may have an advantage over certain other forms of doing business when it comes to attracting and retaining key employees.

Future options. The management of a publicly held corporation generally has more options with regard to future financing of company activities once past the initial public-offering stage.

Less review time. The SEC review of the S-B offering generally does not take as long as its review of the S-1 offering since the S-B filing is effected at the nearest SEC regional office instead of in Washington, D.C., and there is usually less backlog at the regional office.

Disadvantages

Securities attorney. The assistance of (and expense associated with the services of) an experienced securities attorney will undoubtedly be required to mount this level of securities offering.

More expensive overall. In addition to the attorney fees, the other expenses associated with a public securities offering are (1) printing and binding of disclosure documents, (2) accounting fees, (3) broker/dealer commissions and/or fees and (4) other marketing costs that are generally higher than SCOR, Regulation A or private placement securities offerings.

More time consuming. It will generally take more time to "get on the street" with a Regulation S-B offering than a SCOR, Regulation A or private placement offering.

Management flexibility. Publicly held companies have less flexibility in management.

Loss of control. In the instance of a corporation, corporate insiders may lose control of the company if enough of the corporation's shares are sold to the public.

Film company IPOs. Few, if any, feature film production companies have successfully conducted an *initial public offering* of stock in recent years, a situation that results more from the inability of the securities issuers to provide any assurances that they can resolve existing problems with feature film distributor business practices than the actual form of doing business or the form of the securities offering.

Further Reading

Blue Sky Laws—A Course Handbook. Jack H. Halperin and F. Lee Liebolt, Jr. Practicing Law Institute, 1990.

"Commissions to Non-Broker/Dealers Under California Law." Elena R. Freshman. *Beverly Hills Bar Journal* 22, no. 2 (1988).

"Entertainment Finance 1990: Entering a Brave New World." Robert Marich. *The Hollywood Reporter* (Entertainment Finance Special Report), p. F-3, August 1990.

Film Finance and Distribution—A Dictionary of Terms. John W. Cones. Silman-James Press, 1992.

Film Industry Contracts. John W. Cones. Self-published, 1993.

Going Public—Practice, Procedure and Consequences. Carl W. Schneider, Joseph M. Manko, and Robert S. Kant. Bowne, May 1988.

"Hollywood IPOs Net $400 Mil in '91." Jeffrey Daniels. *The Hollywood Reporter*, p. 16, January 3, 1992.

Now That You Are Publicly Owned. . . . Carl W. Schneider and Jason M. Shargel. Bowne, August 1983.

"Recent Developments Concerning Small Company Capital Formation." Wayne Simons. *Beverly Hills Bar Journal*, Spring 1993.

Regulation S-B—Under the Securities Act of 1933 and the Securities Exchange Act of 1934. Bowne, April 1, 1993.

The Securities Law of Public Finance. Robert A. Fippinger. Practicing Law Institute, 1988.

Securities Underwriting: A Practitioner's Guide. Edited by Kenneth J. Bialkin and William J. Grant, Jr. Practicing Law Institute, 1985.

"Taking Stock of Hollywood." Jeffrey Daniels. *The Hollywood Reporter* (Entertainment Special Report), 1992.

"Wall Street Boom Expected to Buoy Small H'wood Firms." Robert Marich. *The Hollywood Reporter*, p. 11, January 10, 1992.

"Wall St. Puts Stock in IPOs—Entertainment Companies Brave Public Waters." Paul Noglows. *Variety*, p. 311, May 4, 1992.

28

S-1 Public (Registered) Offerings

The SEC's Form S-1 is a form of public (registered) securities offering that can be used by feature film producers (and other securities issuers) when a public offering is preferred (as opposed to a private placement) and the issuing organization does not wish to use or does not qualify for the SCOR, Regulation A or Regulation S-B offerings discussed above. The S-1 requires the highest level of disclosure; thus, the prospectus used as the disclosure document in conjunction with an S-1 offering will contain more information or more detailed information, generally speaking, than the other forms of securities offerings. This in turn means that the level of expertise required of the securities attorney is a bit higher than that required for the S-B or other public offerings, and the cost of that expertise may also be reflected in higher attorney's fees.

There is no ceiling on the amount of money that can be raised through the S-1 offerings, but since the S-B form of securities registration permits the issuing entity to have revenues up to $25 million and imposes no specific limit on the amount of money that can be raised, it is unlikely that a feature film producer seeking to raise funds for a single motion picture would have to resort to an S-1 offering. On the other hand, if the producer is seeking to fund the production budgets for a slate of motion pictures or to finance the activities of a corporate production company, the S-1 may prove to be the most useful form of securities registration available.

Like the Regulation S-B offering, the S-1 requires that the producer (issuer) provide a disclosure document (prospectus) to each prospective investor prior to the investment and the regulation sets out in fairly rigorous detail the kinds of information that must be included in the disclosure document. For example, the following information must be provided (this is not a complete list of the S-1 disclosure requirements):

- A description of the business of the issuer (including form and year of organization)
- A statement declaring whether the issuer is a party to any pending legal proceedings
- Certain financial statements of existing companies
- The issuer's directors, executive officers or upper-level management
- Management compensation in all forms
- Specific information that must appear on the outside front cover of the prospectus
- A summary of the prospectus (under some circumstances)
- A discussion of any factors that make the offering speculative or risky (risk factors)
- A statement regarding how the net proceeds of the offering will be used (use of proceeds)
- The issuer's plan for selling the securities (plan of distribution of the securities)
- Certain exhibits such as existing material contracts and attorney's opinions (under some circumstances)
- Other special disclosures relating specifically to the nature of the issuing entity, that is, whether corporation or limited partnership

The primary difference between the S-1 and S-B offerings lies in the area of financial reporting. The S-1 will generally require more financial information relating to the issuing company and covering a longer period of time than the S-B.

The S-1 registration statement, prospectus and exhibits have to be filed with the Washington, D.C., office of the SEC rather than the regional office as with the S-B or Regulation A offerings. Thus, it is generally true that the SEC review of the S-1 will take longer to complete than the other types of offerings.

Financial projections. As with the S-B offerings, the SEC now encourages the use of management's projections of future economic performance in conjunction with public offerings like the Regulation S-1 provisions. However, the SEC does require that such financial projections have a reasonable basis and that they be presented in an appropriate format (as prescribed by the SEC).

Advantages

Advertising permitted. A public (registered) offering such as a Regulation S-1 offering permits advertising to the general public and marketing techniques that fall under the label *general solicitation.*

No ceiling. There is no ceiling on the amount of money that can be raised through an S-1 public (registered) offering.

Key employees. A publicly held corporation may have an advantage in attracting and retaining key employees.

Future options. In the case of a publicly held corporation, its management generally has more options with regard to future financing of company activities once past the initial public-offering stage.

Disadvantages

Securities attorney. The assistance of (and expense associated with the services of) an experienced securities attorney will undoubtedly be required to mount this level of securities offering.

Compared to Form S-B offerings. A Regulation S-1 offering is somewhat more burdensome than a Form S-B securities offering (see chapter 27).

More expensive overall. In addition to the attorney fees, the other expenses associated with a public securities offering are (1) printing and binding of disclosure documents, (2) accounting fees, (3) broker/dealer commissions and/or fees and (4) other marketing costs that are generally higher than SCOR, Regulation A or private placement securities offerings.

More time consuming. It will generally take more time to "get on the street" with a Regulation S-1 offering than a SCOR, Regulation A, S-B offering or private placements.

Management flexibility. Publicly held companies have less flexibility in management than private companies.

Loss of control. In the instance of a corporation, corporate insiders may lose control of the company if enough of the corporation's shares are sold to the public. This control issue has been an ongoing battleground in the film industry ever since the early major studio/distributors began going public.

Further Reading

Blue Sky Laws—A Course Handbook. Jack H. Halperin and F. Lee Liebolt, Jr. Practicing Law Institute, 1990.

"Commissions to Non-Broker/Dealers Under California Law." Elena R. Freshman. *Beverly Hills Bar Journal* 22, no. 2 (1988).

Corporate Forms I—Under the Securities Act of 1933. Bowne, January 1, 1993.

"Entertainment Finance 1990: Entering a Brave New World." Robert Marich. *The Hollywood Reporter* (Entertainment Finance Special Report), p. F-3, August 1990.

Film Finance and Distribution—A Dictionary of Terms. John W. Cones. Silman-James Press, 1992.

Film Industry Contracts. John W. Cones. Self-published, 1993.

"Financing Film and Television Productions—Global Opportunities Emerging in the 1990's." Bruce St. J Lilliston. *Los Angeles Lawyer*, April 1990.

Going Public—Practice, Procedure and Consequences. Carl W. Schneider, Joseph M. Manko, and Robert S. Kant. Bowne, May 1988.

Now That You Are Publicly Owned. . . . Carl W. Schneider and Jason M. Shargel. Bowne, August 1983.

"Recent Developments Concerning Small Company Capital Formation." Wayne Simons. *Beverly Hills Bar Journal*, Spring 1993.

The Securities Law of Public Finance. Robert A. Fippinger. Practicing Law Institute, 1988.

Securities: Public and Private Offerings Rev. ed. William M. Prifti. Callaghan, 1983.

Securities Underwriting: A Practitioner's Guide. Edited by Kenneth J. Bialkin and William J. Grant, Jr. Practicing Law Institute, 1985.

"So You Think You Want to Go Public. . . . " Jay Shapiro. *The Hollywood Reporter. The Securities Law of Public Finance.* Robert A. Fippinger. Practicing Law Institute, 1988.

"Tide of H'wood Investment Rising—Stock Offerings Buoy Industry to the Tune of $3.24 Billion." Robert Marich and Jeffrey Daniels. *The Hollywood Reporter*, August 15, 1991.

"Wall Street on the Pacific—Investment Gurus Multiply in Hollywood's Backyard." Robert Marich and Jeffrey Daniels. *The Hollywood Reporter* (Entertainment Finance Special Report), January 29, 1993.

"Wall St. Puts Stock in IPOs—Entertainment Companies Brave Public Waters." Paul Noglows. *Variety*, p. 311, May 4, 1992.

"What? Quit Show Business?" Alex Ben Block. *Forbes*, August 11, 1986.

"Where the Money Is." *The Hollywood Reporter* (Entertainment Finance Special Report), January 29, 1993.

29

Over-the-Counter Companies

A publicly held film production company may arrange to trade its securities (i.e., arrange to have its securities bought and sold) in several ways. The securities of an over-the-counter (OTC) company are not listed and traded on an organized exchange. The over-the-counter market is a securities market created by dealers who primarily handle trading in securities that are not listed stocks on an organized exchange. OTC trading differs from exchange trading in that transactions are carried out through a telephone/computer network and negotiations with a number of dealers, called market makers, as compared to the single-specialist, single-location auction market mechanism used for listed securities trading. In addition, the market maker acts as principal in the transaction, which involves the dealer as buyer and seller from his or her own inventory.

Some financial observers would suggest that trading a company's securities in the over-the-counter market implies that there is not much interest in the securities; however, OTC trading can reasonably be interpreted to mean that the company has simply chosen not to be listed on an exchange and thus seeks to exercise more control over the market for its securities. A number of broker/dealers in the OTC market may express interest in a particular company's securities with the result that they compete more vigorously to get the best possible price for their customers (or themselves) and this competition in turn benefits the company whose securities are being bought and sold.

From a governmental regulatory standpoint, the OTC market is primarily regulated by the SEC and to some extent by the securities regulatory authority in each state. However, the OTC market is also regulated in a certain sense by the broker/dealer's interest in the security (governed by the supply and demand of customers for the security). Erratic price movements may become the subject of SEC inquiry for facts to justify the activity. Active markets in the OTC sector generally result from the public (registered) offerings that have been the subject of SEC filings.

Advantages

Fewer regulations. OTC trading imposes fewer regulations on a public company than the NASDAQ market (see chapter 30) or the stock exchanges.

More control. A company may be able to exercise more control over the market for its securities through the OTC market than through the stock exchanges.

Disadvantages

Less visibility. The OTC market does not provide a company's stock or other securities with as much visibility as listings on the NASDAQ system or the stock exchanges.

Not much interest. OTC trading may suggest that there is less interest in the securities of an OTC company.

Further Reading

Film Finance and Distribution—A Dictionary of Terms. John W. Cones. Silman-James Press, 1992.

Film Industry Contracts. John W. Cones. Self-published, 1993.

Going Public—Practice, Procedure and Consequences. Carl W. Schneider, Joseph M. Manko, and Robert S. Kant. Bowne, May 1988.

NASD Manual. Commerce Clearing House, September 1990.

Now That You Are Publicly Owned. . . . Carl W. Schneider and Jason M. Shargel. Bowne, August 1983.

"Recent Developments Concerning Small Company Capital Formation." Wayne Simons. *Beverly Hills Bar Journal*, Spring 1993.

The Securities Law of Public Finance. Robert A. Fippinger. Practicing Law Institute, 1988.

Securities: Public and Private Offerings. Rev. ed. William M. Prifti. Callaghan, 1983.

30

A NASDAQ Company

NASDAQ is the acronym for the National Association of Securities Dealers Automated Quotations, a national automated quotation service for over-the-counter securities. Operation of the NASDAQ system is supervised by the National Association of Securities Dealers (NASD), and informational input is provided by hundreds of over-the-counter market makers. Market makers are securities broker/dealers who make a market for a given security; that is, such firms maintain a firm bid and offer price on a given security by standing ready to buy or sell round lots at publicly quoted prices. A managing underwriter typically makes a market for its client's stock.

In order to qualify for inclusion in the NASDAQ system, a security must satisfy numerous requirements. For example, for initial inclusion in the NASDAQ system,

- the issue must have two registered and active market makers;
- the issuer must have total assets of at least $2 million;
- the issuer must have capital and surplus of at least $1 million;
- in the case of a convertible debt security, there must be a principal amount outstanding of at least $10 million;
- in the case of common stock, there must be at least 300 holders of the security and at least 100,000 publicly held shares;
- in the case of rights and warrants, there must be at least 100,000 issued;
- the security must not be under a current SEC trading suspension;
- the issuer has to pay a NASDAQ Issuer Quotation fee;
- the issuer has to file with the NASD three copies of all reports and other documents filed or required to be filed with the SEC; and
- the companies' annual reports filed with the NASD must contain audited financial statements.

Many persons in the securities industry feel the NASDAQ system has resulted in significant improvements in the over-the-counter securities market. NASDAQ has made available electronic price quotations and trading volume information for a significant number of over-the-counter securities. Many newspapers currently carry the NASDAQ National List of securities, which has similar financial criteria to those of the American Stock Exchange. Some of the newspapers also publish the Additional List of NASDAQ securities, which is based on the dollar value of share volume. The total number of shares traded on the NASDAQ market now exceeds that of the American Stock Exchange. An actively traded NASDAQ security supported by several market makers may (1) command more broker/dealer interest, (2) have a larger trading volume and (3) develop more market depth than many stocks listed on the exchanges. As a result, many NASDAQ-traded companies no longer seek exchange listing when they become eligible for such listing, preferring to remain in the NASDAQ market.

Advantages

Instant availability. The NASDAQ market makes the securities of qualifying companies instantly available for trading by broker/dealers all across the country, which may facilitate rapid capitalization.

Eligibility requirements. The NASDAQ eligibility requirements are generally less burdensome than the requirements of the major stock exchanges.

Disadvantages

More mature companies. The NASDAQ market is generally only suitable for more mature companies with sophisticated management and the capability of paying significant professional fees to accountants and attorneys qualified to supervise such transactions.

Eligibility requirements. The NASDAQ eligibility requirements are generally more burdensome than general OTC requirements.

Further Reading

Film Finance and Distribution—A Dictionary of Terms. John W. Cones. Silman-James Press, 1992.
Film Industry Contracts. John W. Cones. Self-published, 1993.
Going Public—Practice, Procedure and Consequences. Carl W. Schneider, Joseph M. Manko, and Robert S. Kant. Bowne, May 1988.
NASD Manual. Commerce Clearing House, September 1990.

Now That You Are Publicly Owned. . . . Carl W. Schneider and Jason M. Shargel. Bowne, August 1983.

"Recent Developments Concerning Small Company Capital Formation." Wayne Simons. *Beverly Hills Bar Journal*, Spring 1993.

The Securities Law of Public Finance. Robert A. Fippinger. Practicing Law Institute, 1988.

Securities: Public and Private Offerings. Rev. ed. William M. Prifti. Callaghan, 1983.

31

Stock Exchange Companies

The national securities exchanges provide a convenient marketplace for their member broker/dealer firms to execute buy and sell orders for customers. However, a film production (or other) company's securities can be traded on a specific exchange only after meeting the exchange's listing requirements. After meeting those requirements, a broker/dealer (a so-called specialist) is assigned to make an orderly market in the security. In other words, it is the responsibility of the specialist to match buy and sell orders for the production company's securities and generally maintain some degree of liquidity in the company's securities.

The two major stock exchanges (the New York Stock Exchange and the American Stock Exchange) maintain certain policies that have to be considered by any company before making the decision to list on either exchange. Those policies are set forth in the respective New York and American Stock Exchange guides, which may be obtained from those exchanges. Such policies relate to conflicts of interest, voting rights, the requiring of shareholder votes in certain situations, outside directors, audit committees, controls relating to the future issuance of a company's stock and the timely public release of important corporation developments. Most of the policies are articulated as general guides for the conduct of their respective listed companies, and the guides are applied on a case-by-case basis, depending on the individual facts. Even if a film production or other company decides not to apply for listing on an exchange, those well-established exchange policies may serve as useful guides to good corporate practice—even for over-the-counter companies.

The exchanges regulate themselves and their specialists with rules approved by the SEC. Price movement greater than a specified amount (e.g., over one-fourth of a point) or other unusual price movements may require approval of a floor governor or the exchange, as well as general publicity intended to offer an explanation.

Listing on some of the stock exchanges may provide for automatic securities registration in certain states. The securities laws of each state (blue-sky laws) in which the security is intended to be offered or sold should be reviewed to determine whether exchange listing brings automatic state registration.

If a film production company can meet the listing requirements of the New York Stock Exchange, it is generally regarded as highly desirable to do so. However, only a few companies can typically meet the listing requirements of the New York Stock Exchange after a single public offering of their securities. If a film production company can meet the somewhat lower listing requirements of the American Stock Exchange, it may choose to do so. Some issuers, however, prefer to *season* (mature in the marketplace) their securities with a brief period of over-the-counter trading before the listing on the exchange is completed (see chapter 29).

Small public issues of corporate film production company securities may be listed on the regional stock exchanges. The principal regional exchanges are located in Boston, Detroit, Chicago (the Midwest Stock Exchange), Philadelphia and Los Angeles (the Pacific Stock Exchange, which actually maintains facilities in both Los Angeles and San Francisco).

The exchanges generally do not have regulations concerning the underwriting of over-the-counter securities by member firms (see chapter 29).

Advantages

Prestige. Listing on a stock exchange may create more prestige for a film production company in the eyes of investors, customers and suppliers.

Employee considerations. A film production company whose stock is listed on an exchange may appear to be more attractive to new employees.

Acquisitions. Stock exchange listing of a company's securities may facilitate the acquisition of the company by another firm.

Collateral Value. Security listed on a stock exchange will generally have a higher and more readily ascertainable collateral value in the event that the investor wishes to borrow funds using the security as collateral.

Press releases. Stock exchange listing generally increases a company's ability to get its press releases and quotations more widely disseminated by the news media.

Value of specialist. The stock exchange listing typically obligates the specialist to make a fair and orderly market for the security by purchasing it and selling it for the specialist's own account if necessary.

State preferential treatment. Generally speaking, listing on a stock exchange will qualify a company's securities for preferential treatment by the state securities regulators.

More stable prices. There is generally less volatility in the price of a company's securities when those securities are listed on a stock exchange rather than being traded in the over-the-counter market.

Closer spreads. The *spread* (difference between the bid and offered quotations on a security) is typically not as great on listed securities as on securities traded in the OTC market.

Disadvantages

Listing requirements. Many companies cannot meet the listing requirements to become an exchange company.

OTC trading. Over-the-counter trading of a company's securities may prove to be more advantageous to a particular company than a listing on some of the exchanges.

Exchange policies. Certain of the exchange policies may prove too burdensome for some smaller companies.

Further Reading

"Entertainment Finance 1990: Entering a Brave New World." Robert Marich. *The Hollywood Reporter* (Entertainment Finance Special Report), p. F-3, August 1990.

Film Finance and Distribution—A Dictionary of Terms. John W. Cones. Silman-James Press, 1992.

Film Industry Contracts. John W. Cones. Self-published, 1993.

"Film Profits Lag Industry, Survey Says." Linda Keslar. *Variety*, November 23, 1992.

Going Public—Practice, Procedure and Consequences. Carl W. Schneider, Joseph M. Manko, and Robert S. Kant. Bowne, May 1988.

"Hollywood's Top-45 Public Companies—Ranked By Sales." *The Hollywood Reporter* (Entertainment Finance Special Report), 1992.

"IPO's Raise a Record $39.4 Billion for '92." Sara Calian. *Wall Street Journal*, January 4, 1993.

NASD Manual. Commerce Clearing House, September 1990.

Now That You Are Publicly Owned. . . . Carl W. Schneider and Jason M. Shargel. Bowne, August 1983.

The Securities Law of Public Finance. Robert A. Fippinger. Practicing Law Institute, 1988.

Securities: Public and Private Offerings Rev. ed. William M. Prifti. Callaghan, 1983.

Understanding the Securities Laws. Larry D. Soderquist. Practicing Law Institute, 1990.

"Vision Quest—Wall Street Sees the Future in Media." *Journal of Entertainment Finance*, September/October 1993.

"Wall Street on the Pacific—Investment Gurus Multiply in Hollywood's Backyard." Robert Marich and Jeffrey Daniels. *The Hollywood Reporter* (Entertainment Finance Special Report), January 29, 1993.

"Where the Money Is." *The Hollywood Reporter* (Entertainment Finance Special Report), January 29, 1993.

32

Convertible or Participatory Debt Instruments

The convertible or participatory debt instrument is a hybrid security that offers some characteristics of corporate stock and some features of corporate bonds. It is like stock in that the total rate of return on the instrument is tied to the future performance of the company or a specific project, and it is like a bond in that it pays a stated rate of interest. The return on a convertible security is linked to the company's earnings, which to a large degree will determine the price at which the stock trades. The return for a participatory security will generally be tied to the performance of a specific project.

Convertible securities. Convertible securities are corporate financial instruments that are exchangeable for a set number of another form of corporate ownership, that is, common stock, at a prestated price. Convertible securities usually take the form of preferred stock or bonds—a debt instrument. They are most appropriate for investors who want higher income than is available from common stock, together with greater appreciation potential than regular bonds offer. From the issuer's standpoint, the convertible feature is usually designed as a sweetener to enhance the marketability of the stock or bond.

Corporate bonds. Corporate bonds are interest-bearing or discounted corporate securities that obligate the issuer to pay the bondholder a specified sum of money, usually at specific intervals, and to repay the principal amount of the loan at maturity. Bondholders, in effect, have an IOU from the corporate issuer but no corporate ownership privileges, such as those stockholders possess.

Debt security. A debt security is a security representing money borrowed that must be repaid and having a fixed amount, a specific maturity or maturities, and usually a specific rate of interest or an original purchase disco nt, for example, a bill, bond, commercial paper or note.

Participatory debt ir strument. A participatory debt instrument is a hybrid security tha , in addition to debt features, also provides equity participation, th t is, the right to participate with common stockholders in additior al distributions of earnings under specified conditions.

Advantages

No dilution. The u e of such instruments does allow a feature film production compar y organized as a corporation to raise funds without diluting the pre sent shareholder's equity ownership in the company.

Lower interest rates The interest on these instruments will typically be lower than that produced by conventional debt alternatives, such as a bank loan or a nother kind of bond.

Institutional investo s. Such instruments may also appeal to institutional investors.

Disadvantages

Interest. Like a bo d, the security will be carried on the company's books as debt, ar d interest will have to be paid.

Securities law com liance. In most instances, the above-described financial instru nents are securities, and thus the producer will have to comply witt both the applicable federal and state securities laws.

Public companies. Generally speaking, an offering of such instruments will work onl 7 for corporate entities, namely, film production companies organize d as corporations, and generally only for corporations that have go e public, that is, whose shares have been previously offered in a public/registered securities offering and are thus publicly held.

Investment bankers A public offering of convertible or participatory debt instrume its will in all likelihood require the involvement of a national or re gional investment banking firm and a securities attorney represent ing the film producer. Unless a significant amount of money is bei g raised, it may not be economically feasible to pay their fees, along with other costs of conducting such an exotic offering.

141

Further Reading

Film Finance and Distribution—A Dictionary of Terms. John W. Cones. Silman-James Press, 1992.

Film Industry Contracts. John W. Cones. Self-published, 1993.

Financing Dreams into Reality. Richard L. Intrator. Ernst and Young, Summer 1989.

"Investors Get Their Kicks Out of Show Business." Robert Marich. *The Hollywood Reporter* (Entertainment Finance Special Report), p. S-24, January 1991.

Understanding the Securities Laws. Larry D. Soderquist. Practicing Law Institute, 1990.

33

Regulation D, Rule 504 Offerings

Regulation D is an SEC exemption from the securities registration requirement. In other words, if a feature film producer wants to raise money from passive investors, the interests in whatever vehicle or entity is created for that purpose are most likely going to be securities (corporate stocks, limited partnership interests, passive investor percentage participations, etc.); thus, the producer must comply with both the federal and the state securities laws. One of the foremost requirements of those laws is that the issuer register its securities with the SEC at the federal level and with the appropriate state regulatory authorities in each state in which such securities are going to be offered or sold (these registered offerings are also referred to as public offerings). In the alternative, the issuer may wish to comply with available exemptions from the securities registration requirement, and the exemptions (more specifically, the transactional exemptions) are commonly referred to as *private placements, private placement exemptions, exempt offerings, nonpublic offering exemptions* or (at the state level) *limited offering exemptions* and *small offering exemptions.*

Regulation D is simply one of several exemptions available at the federal level. Sections 4(2) and 4(6) of the 1933 Securities Act are also considered private placement exemptions, as well as Section 3(a)(11) of the same Act, although Regulation D is by far the most commonly relied-upon exemption. Thus, the others named above are not discussed in this presentation (see Introduction). Rule 504 is just one of three different specific sets of rules within Regulation D that permit issuers to sell securities in a nonpublic offering, that is, in a private placement.

In order for a film production company (or other securities issuer) to qualify for the transactional exemption for one of its securities offerings pursuant to Rule 504, the offers and sales must satisfy the general terms and conditions of Regulation D relating to

143

- treating a single offering as a series of offerings to avoid application of the rules (securities integration);
- disclosing prescribed information to prospective investors (information requirements);
- complying with the general prohibition against advertising and general solicitation (limitations on the manner of offering—limitations that as a practical matter mean sales can only be made to persons with whom upper-level management of the issuing entity had a preexisting relationship, that is, prior to the start of the offering);
- complying with provisions that limit the resale of such securities by the original investors (limitations on resale); and
- filing the required Form D in a timely manner (filing of notice of sales).

Ceiling on amount of money. Rule 504 further imposes a limit on the aggregate offering price (or amount of money that can be raised) in reliance on this specific rule; that is, not more than $1 million can be raised pursuant to Rule 504 within a twelve-month period.

Number of investors. There is no limit on the number of investors who can invest in a Rule 504 offering. However, since the securities issuer must comply with both the federal and the state securities laws and since most compatible state private placement (or limited offering) exemptions do impose limits on the number of investors, this provision of Rule 504 is generally of little value. The ceiling on the number of investors imposed by the state law controls the number of investors in such situations.

Specific disclosure requirements. Rule 504 also provides that "the issuer is not required to furnish the specified information to purchasers when it sells securities under Rule 504." However, this provision is often misinterpreted to mean that a Rule 504 offering does not require the preparation and presentation of a disclosure document (offering memorandum) to each prospective investor. Nothing could be further from the truth since the Preliminary Notes to Regulation D clearly state that transactions conducted in accordance with Regulation D "are not exempt from the anti-fraud . . . provisions of the Federal securities laws" and the antifraud provisions require that issuers of securities disclose in writing to all prospective investors all material aspects of the transaction, that they not leave out any material information and that they must present the information in a manner that is not misleading to the prospective investors. A violation of the antifraud rules could result in securities fraud; thus, a complete disclosure document is still required for a Rule 504 offering. The safer practice, in the view of some securities attorneys, is to rely for guidance on the specific disclosure guidelines provided for the next highest level of exempt offering (the Rule 505 exemption).

Issuer disqualifiers. Unlike Rule 505 (see chapter 34), Rule 504 does not impose the set of so-called issuer disqualifiers on those persons who would seek to sell securities under Rule 504. The disqualifiers basically state that the exemption is not available to persons who have been guilty of certain securities law or other violations within the most recent five years. Again, however, most of the state exemptions that would need to be complied with by an issuer relying on Rule 504 do impose similar issuer disqualifiers; therefore, the producer must carefully review those disqualifying provisions and be familiar with the backgrounds of persons involved in the selling of the offering.

Advantages

Disclosure less burdensome. The antifraud rules presumably allow a bit more leeway with respect to disclosure than the more specific disclosure guidelines of a Rule 505 offering.

Faster than public offerings. A private placement generally allows the producer to put together a disclosure document and be "on the street" raising money more quickly than a public (registered) offering.

No advance regulatory approval required. The private placement disclosure document does not have to be submitted to the SEC or state regulatory authorities for approval prior to its use with prospective investors as in public (registered) offerings.

Less expensive. Private placements are generally less expensive to mount than public offerings.

Disadvantages

Disclosure mistakes could be costly. A mistake in judgment with respect to disclosure when merely trying to comply with the very general antifraud rule as opposed to the more specific Rule 505 disclosure guidelines could result in securities fraud.

Funding limit. A Rule 504 offering only permits the producer to raise $1 million.

Preexisting relationship. In contrast to a public (registered) offering, securities being offered pursuant to any Regulation D (private placement) exemption can only be offered as a general rule to persons with whom upper-level management of the issuing entity has a preexisting relationship (i.e., before the start of the offering).

Complex securities laws. The complexity of the securities laws makes it almost imperative that an experienced securities attorney be engaged, preferably with experience in film or film company offerings, and attorney fees can be relatively expensive for start-up production companies.

State law compliance required. In addition to complying with the federal securities laws and regulations, issuers of securities must also comply with the applicable state securities laws and regulations (blue-sky laws) in each state in which those securities are to be offered or sold.

Further Reading

Blue Sky Law. Joseph C. Long. Clark Boardman, 1986.

Blue Sky Law Reporter. Commerce Clearing House (updated every two weeks).

Blue Sky Laws—A Course Handbook. Jack H. Halperin and F. Lee Liebolt, Jr. Practicing Law Institute, 1990.

Film and Video Financing. Michael Wiese. Michael Wiese Productions, 1991.

Film Finance and Distribution—A Dictionary of Terms. John W. Cones. Silman-James Press, 1992.

Film Industry Contracts. John W. Cones. Self-published, 1993.

Financing Your Film—A Guide for Independent Filmmakers and Producers. Trisha Curran, Praeger Publishers, 1986.

Going Public—Practice, Procedure and Consequences. Carl W. Schneider, Joseph M. Manko, and Robert S. Kant. Bowne, May 1988.

Independent Feature Film Production—A Complete Guide from Concept to Distribution. Gregory Goodell. St. Martin's Press, 1982.

NASD Manual. Commerce Clearing House. September 1990.

Now That You Are Publicly Owned. . . . Carl W. Schneider and Jason M. Shargel. Bowne, August 1983.

"Private Placements Come Out of the Closet." Robert Marich. *The Hollywood Reporter* (Entertainment Finance Special Report), p. S-4, January 1991.

Producing, Financing and Distributing Film—A Comprehensive Legal and Business Guide. 2d ed. Paul A. Baumgarten, Donald C. Farber, and Mark Fleischer. Limelight Editions, 1992.

"Recent Developments Concerning Small Company Capital Formation." Wayne Simons. *Beverly Hills Bar Journal*, Spring 1993.

Regulation D—Rules 501 Through 508. Bowne, January 1, 1993.

Securities: Public and F rivate Offerings. Rev. ed. William M. Prifti. Callaghan, 1983.

Understanding the Securi ies Laws. Larry D. Soderquist. Practicing Law Institute, 1990.

34

Regulation D, Rule 505 Offerings

Rule 505 is the second of the three specific sets of rules within the SEC's (federal) Regulation D that permit issuers to sell securities in a nonpublic offering, that is, in private placements (see chapter 33).

Just as with Rule 504, a feature film production company (or other issuer) seeking to qualify for the transactional exemption for one of its securities offerings pursuant to Regulation D, Rule 505, must satisfy the general terms and conditions of Regulation D in the conduct of its offers and sales as those terms and conditions relate to

- treating a single offering as a series of offerings to avoid application of the rules (securities integration);
- disclosing information to prospective investors (information requirements);
- complying with the general prohibition against advertising and general solicitation (limitations on the manner of offering—limitations that as a practical matter mean sales can only be made to persons with whom upper-management of the issuing entity had a preexisting relationship, that is, prior to the start of the offering);
- complying with provisions that limit the resale of such securities by the original investors (limitations on resale); and
- filing the required Form D in a timely manner (filing of notice of sales).

Ceiling on amount of money. Rule 505, however, relaxes the ceiling on the amount of money that can be raised to some extent. The Rule 505 limitation on the aggregate offering price is $5 million; again, that amount must be raised in a twelve-month period.

Number of investors. Rule 505 utilizes a different approach than Rule 504 with respect to the number of investors that may be permitted to invest in such an offering. No more than thirty-five nonaccredited investors are allowed pursuant to Rule 505, but an unlimited number of accredited investors are permitted. There are eight kinds of accredited investors defined in Regulation D. However, film producers are most likely to be making offers to only two categories: (1) natural persons whose individual net worth or joint net worth with that person's spouse at the time of purchase exceeds $1 million; or (2) natural persons who had an individual income in excess of $200,000 in each of the two most recent years or joint income with that person's spouse in excess of $300,000 in each of those years and who has a reasonable expectation of reaching the same income level in the current year.

Specific disclosure requirements. Unlike Rule 504, Rule 505 provides specific disclosure guidelines. Those disclosure guidelines are tied to the specific guidelines of the public offerings pursuant to Regulation A or Regulation S-B, depending on the amount of money being raised (see chapters 26 and 27).

Issuer disqualifiers. Rule 505 imposes a set of so-called issuer disqualifiers on those persons who would seek to sell securities under Rule 505. The disqualifiers basically state that the exemption is not available to persons who have been guilty of certain securities law or other violations within the most recent five years. Thus, if a producer allows persons who are disqualified to sell the production company's securities, the exemption from registration may be voided, leaving the producer in the awkward position of having sold an unregistered security an activity that might involve both civil and criminal penalties.

Advantages

Disclosure less burdensome. The disclosures required (i.e., the kind of information that must be put in writing in an offering memorandum) for a Rule 505 offering are somewhat less burdensome than those required for a Rule 506 offering.

Easier compliance. It is easier to comply with the more specific disclosure guidelines imposed by Rule 505 than the less specific anti-fraud rules imposed on Rule 504 offerings.

Higher level of funding allowed. Compared with Rule 504 offering, the Rule 505 exemption permits the raising of five times more money—$5 million as opposed to $1 million.

Faster than public offerings. A private placement (including the Regulation D, Rule 505 offering) generally allows the producer to put together a disclosure document and be "on the street" raising money more quickly than a public (registered) offering. Actually raising the money may take just as much time, depending on other factors.

Less expensive. Private placements are generally less expensive to mount than public offerings.

Disadvantages

Funding limit. A Rule 505 offering only permits the producer to raise $5 million, unlike the Rule 506 offering that imposes no ceiling on the aggregate offering price.

Preexisting relationship. In contrast to a public (registered) offering, securities being offered pursuant to any Regulation D (private placement) exemption can only be offered to persons with whom upper-level management of the issuing entity has a preexisting relationship (i.e., before the start of the offering).

Complex securities laws. The complexity of the securities laws makes it almost imperative that an experienced securities attorney be engaged, preferably with experience in film or film company offerings, and attorney fees can be relatively expensive for start-up production companies.

State law compliance required. In addition to complying with the federal securities laws and regulations, issuers of securities must also comply with the applicable state securities laws and regulations (blue-sky laws) in each state in which the securities are to be offered or sold.

Further Reading

Blue Sky Law. Joseph C. Long. Clark Boardman, 1986.

Blue Sky Law Reporter. Commerce Clearing House (updated every two weeks).

Blue Sky Laws—A Course Handbook. Jack H. Halperin and F. Lee Liebolt, Jr. Practicing Law Institute, 1990.

"Entertainment Finance 1990: Entering a Brave New World." Robert Marich. *The Hollywood Reporter* (Entertainment Finance Special Report), p. F-3, August 1990.

Film and Video Financing. Michael Wiese. Michael Wiese Productions, 1991.

Film Finance and Distribution—A Dictionary of Terms. John W. Cones. Silman-James Press, 1992.

Film Industry Contracts. John W. Cones. Self-published, 1993.

Financing Your Film—A Guide for Independent Filmmakers and Producers. Trisha Curran. Praeger Publishers, 1986.

Going Public—Practice, Procedure and Consequences. Carl W. Schneider, Joseph M. Manko, and Robert S. Kant. Bowne, May 1988.

Independent Feature Film Production—A Complete Guide from Concept to Distribution. Gregory Goodell. St. Martin's Press, 1982.

"Investors Get Their Kicks out of Show Business." Robert Marich. *The Hollywood Reporter* (Entertainment Finance Special Report), p. S-24, January 1991.

NASD Manual. Commerce Clearing House. September 1990.

Now That You Are Publicly Owned. . . . Carl W. Schneider and Jason M. Shargel. Bowne, August 1983.

"Private Placements Come Out of the Closet." Robert Marich. *The Hollywood Reporter* (Entertainment Finance Special Report), p. S-4, January 1991.

Producing, Financing and Distributing Film—A Comprehensive Legal and Business Guide. 2d ed. Paul A. Baumgarten, Donald C. Farber, and Mark Fleischer. Limelight Editions, 1992.

"Recent Developments Concerning Small Company Capital Formation." Wayne Simons. *Beverly Hills Bar Journal*, Spring 1993.

Regulation D—Rules 501 Through 508. Bowne, January 1, 1993.

Securities: Public and Private Offerings. Rev. ed. William M. Prifti. Callaghan, 1983.

Understanding the Securities Laws. Larry D. Soderquist. Practicing Law Institute, 1990.

35

Regulation D, Rule 506 Offerings

Rule 506 is the last of the three specific sets of rules within the SEC's (federal) Regulation D that permit issuers to sell securities in a nonpublic offering, that is, in private placements (see chapters 33 and 34).

As with Rules 504 and 505, a feature film production company (or other issuer) seeking to qualify for the transactional exemption for one of its securities offerings pursuant to Regulation D, Rule 506, must satisfy the general terms and conditions of Regulation D in the conduct of its offers and sales as those terms and conditions relate to

- treating a single offering as a series of offerings to avoid application of the rules (securities integration);
- disclosing information to prospective investors (information requirements);
- complying with the general prohibition against advertising and general solicitation (limitations on the manner of offering—limitations that as a practical matter mean sales can only be made to persons with whom upper-management of the issuing entity had a preexisting relationship, that is, prior to the start of the offering);
- complying with provisions that limit the resale of such securities by the original investors (limitations on resale); and
- filing the required Form D in a timely manner (filing of notice of sales).

Ceiling on amount of money. Unlike Rules 505 and 504, Rule 506 does not impose a ceiling on the amount of money that can be raised pursuant to Rule 506.

Number of investors. Rule 506 utilizes the same approach as Rule 505 with respect to the number of investors that may be permitted to invest in the offering. No more than thirty-five nonaccredited investors are allowed pursuant to Rule 506, but an unlimited number of accredited investors are permitted. There are eight different kinds of accredited investors defined in Regulation D. However, film producers are most likely to be making offers to only two categories: (1)

natural persons whose individual net worth or joint net worth with that person's spouse at the time of purchase exceeds $1 million; or (2) natural persons who had an individual income in excess of $200,000 in each of the two most recent years or joint income with that person's spouse in excess of $300,000 in each of those years and who has a reasonable expectation of reaching the same income level in the current year.

Specific disclosure requirements.　Unlike Rule 504 (but like Rule 505), Rule 506 provides specific disclosure guidelines that are tied to specific guidelines of public offerings. The Rule 506 disclosure guidelines correspond to Regulation S-B or S-1, depending on the amount of money being raised (see chapters 27 and 28).

Issuer disqualifiers.　Rule 506 does not impose a set of so-called issuer disqualifiers on those persons who would seek to sell securities under Rule 506. However, compatible state exemptions generally do impose such issuer disqualifiers. Those disqualifiers basically state that the exemption is not available to persons who have been guilty of certain securities law or other violations within the most recent five years. Thus, as in a Rule 505 offering, if a film producer allows persons who are disqualified to sell the production company's securities, the exemption from registration may be voided, leaving the producer in the awkward position of having sold an unregistered security, an activity that might involve both civil and criminal penalties.

Nature of purchasers.　Rule 506 does impose investor suitability standards on investors who are not accredited. Thus, Rule 506 requires that each purchaser who is not an accredited investor either alone or with such purchaser's purchaser representative(s) has such knowledge and experience in financial and business matters that the purchaser is capable of evaluating the merits and risks of the prospective investment. In the alternative, the issuer must reasonably believe immediately prior to making any sale that the purchaser comes within that description. Producers and other securities issuers relying on Regulation D, Rule 506, must therefore inquire as to their nonaccredited investors' financial knowledge and experience by means of the subscription application.

Advantages

No funding limit.　A Rule 506 offering does not impose any ceiling on the amount of money that can be raised pursuant to a Rule 506 offering.

153

Faster than public offerings. A private placement (including the Regulation D, Rule 506 offering) generally allows the producer to put together a disclosure document and be "on the street" raising money more quickly than a public (registered) offering. The actual time it takes to raise the money may be the same, depending on other factors.

Less expensive. Private placements are generally less expensive to mount than public offerings.

Disadvantages

Highest level of disclosure. Rule 506 imposes the highest level of disclosure of the three Regulation D exemptions (see chapters 33 and 34).

Preexisting relationship. In contrast to a public (registered) offering, securities being offered pursuant to any Regulation D (private placement) exemption as a general rule can only be offered to persons with whom upper-level management of the issuing entity had a preexisting relationship (i.e., before the start of the offering).

Complex securities laws. The complexity of the securities laws makes it almost imperative that an experienced securities attorney be engaged, preferably with experience in film or film company offerings, and attorney fees can be relatively expensive for start-up production companies.

State law compliance required. In addition to complying with the federal securities laws and regulations, issuers of securities must also comply with the applicable state securities laws and regulations (blue-sky laws).

Further Reading

Blue Sky Law. Joseph C. Long. Clark Boardman, 1986.

Blue Sky Law Reporter. Commerce Clearing House (updated every two weeks).

Blue Sky Laws—A Course Handbook. Jack H. Halperin and F. Lee Liebolt, Jr. Practicing Law Institute, 1990.

"Entertainment Finance 1990: Entering a Brave New World." Robert Marich. *The Hollywood Reporter* (Entertainment Finance Special Report), p. F-3, August 1990.

Film and Video Financing. Michael Wiese. Michael Wiese Productions, 1991.

Film Finance and Distribution—A Dictionary of Terms. John W. Cones. Silman-James Press, 1992.

Film Industry Contracts. John W. Cones. Self-published, 1993.

"Financing Film and Television Productions—Global Opportunities Emerging in the 1990's." Bruce St. J Lilliston. *Los Angeles Lawyer*, April 1990.

Financing Your Film—A Guide for Independent Filmmakers and Producers. Trisha Curran. Praeger Publishers, 1986.

Going Public—Practice, Procedure and Consequences. Carl W. Schneider, Joseph M. Manko, and Robert S. Kant. Bowne. May 1988.

Independent Feature Film Production—A Complete Guide from Concept to Distribution. Gregory Goodell. St. Martin's Press, 1982.

"Investors Get Their Kicks out of Show Business." Robert Marich. *The Hollywood Reporter* (Entertainment Finance Special Report), p. S-24, January 1991.

NASD Manual. Commerce Clearing House, September 1990.

Now That You Are Publicly Owned. . . . Carl W. Schneider and Jason M. Shargel. Bowne, August 1983.

"Private Placements Come Out of the Closet." Robert Marich. *The Hollywood Reporter* (Entertainment Finance Special Report), p. S-4, January 1991.

Producing, Financing and Distributing Film—A Comprehensive Legal and Business Guide. 2d ed. Paul A. Baumgarten, Donald C. Farber, and Mark Fleischer. Limelight Editions, 1992.

"Recent Developments Concerning Small Company Capital Formation." Wayne Simons. *Beverly Hills Bar Journal,* Spring 1993.

Regulation D—Rules 501 Through 508. Bowne, January 1, 1993.

Securities: Public and Private Offerings. Rev. ed. William M. Prifti. Callaghan, 1983.

Understanding the Securities Laws. Larry D. Soderquist. Practicing Law Institute, 1990.

PART 4

Foreign Financing

36

Blocked Currency or Blocked Funds Deals

Blocked currencies or blocked funds. In some countries, moneys earned by foreign banks or corporations in that country cannot be removed from the country (except under limited circumstances) because of limitations imposed by local law. Thus, generally, such funds have to be spent within the borders of that country producing a product or commodity, which can then be taken out of the country. The currency restrictions are designed to help the local economy. In the film industry, blocked currencies may be foreign film rentals, and often distribution deals will provide that such funds will be deposited in an account in such foreign country for the benefit of the distributor (sometimes for the benefit of the producer).

Restricted currencies Blocked funds are also referred to as *restricted currencies.* Restricted currencies are defined as foreign currencies that are or become subject to moratorium, embargo, banking or exchange restrictions or restrictions against remittances to the United States.

Blocked funds accumulate in the bank accounts of U.S. and foreign companies in foreign countries. The foreign country's laws that prevent the removal of currency will allow the removal of a product produced in that country with such currency. A film will generally qualify as a product produced with the blocked funds in the foreign country and can thus be removed.

Blocked funds deals. So-called blocked funds deals are a variant method of motion picture financing that may be able to provide some below-the-line savings. In a blocked funds deal, a film producer purchases blocked funds or currency at a discounted rate from banks or corporations doing business in a specific country.

Foreign location shoot. A producer seeking to finance the production costs of a motion picture through the use of blocked funds must first determine whether the film can be suitably produced in a foreign country. Then the producer must locate a sufficient amount of

159

blocked funds in the same country that is suitable for the particular production.

Finding blocked funds. In order to locate blocked funds, producers or their representatives should seek to identify and contact specific persons functioning as the treasurers or chief financial officers of U.S. corporations, including film distribution companies, that do a significant amount of business in foreign countries. Major international law firms and the larger commercial banks with specialists in this field may be able to provide useful information and assistance in putting together such deals. Directly contacting the foreign banks holding such funds is not generally productive since the banks themselves would not be able to disclose the name of depositors at the bank with blocked funds.

Narrowing the list. In an effort to narrow the prospects, the producer may first want to determine which foreign countries providing suitable locations and production capabilities for the planned film also impose the limitations on the removal of currency from the country. Then the producer can seek to identify U.S. companies that do a significant amount of business in those countries.

Foreign trade and film commissions. It may be possible to obtain a list of U.S. companies doing business in a given country from the foreign trade commission of that country. Another approach is to contact the film commission in the country the producer may want to shoot the film in and inquire as to whether that country imposes restrictions on the removal of currency from the country and what foreign companies may have blocked funds there (see "Official AFCI Directory" under Further Reading).

Some countries with currency restrictions. Foreign coproduction deals utilizing blocked currencies have been effected in recent years in Russia, Ireland, Yugoslavia and Algeria. Brazil and India also impose strict restrictions on the amount of their currencies that can be converted into U.S. dollars and taken out of the country.

Blocked funds as an equity investment. An alternative, which does not involve the requirement that the producer come up with purchase moneys for blocked funds, is to convince the corporation holding blocked funds to use such funds as an equity investment in the production of the film. However, a company with blocked funds will not typically want to enter into such a deal with a producer who does not have a track record for producing films that generate sufficient funds to allow the company to recover its investment. That tends to narrow the field considerably.

160

Even better when exchange rate is favorable. A blocked funds deal is even more attractive in a country where the U.S. dollar is strong and has a favorable exchange rate with the local currency. A producer should also seek to negotiate a purchase price with the companies holding blocked funds that is more favorable than the official exchange rate. This increases the buying power of the blocked funds in the foreign country; thus, a producer could ostensibly increase the production value of the film even more in such a situation. It is helpful if the producer can find a company that has been sitting on blocked funds in a given country for a number of years. In that situation, the corporation with blocked funds may be anxious to convert those funds into U.S. dollars; in other words, the company holding the blocked funds is a motivated seller.

Advantages

Discounted monies. Blocked funds are available on a discounted basis: for a $1 million investment a producer might be able to produce a $2 million film on location in a foreign country.

In combination with limited partnerships. Blocked funds opportunities may be combined with a feature film limited partnership so that limited partner funds can first be used to purchase blocked funds at a discount and the investor funds are immediately leveraged into greater purchasing power.

Not highly publicized situations. Companies with blocked funds try to be discreet with regard to whom they disclose the existence of their blocked funds. They do not want to be flooded with requests for blocked funds deals. Although that may appear to be a disadvantage at first, it may be considered an advantage for feature film producers since not many producers are likely to be aware of these opportunities; thus, the competition for such monies may be limited.

Disadvantages

Blocked funds cost money. The producer will have to have enough money to purchase the blocked funds at whatever discounted rate they are offered. Sometimes a limited partnership offering may be used to raise the initial producer funds; then as an integral part of the limited partnership strategy, those investor funds can be used to purchase blocked funds at a significant discount.

Production problems. Many of the problems typically associated with any foreign film production will also be encountered in a blocked funds deal, namely, restrictive regulations relating to the cast, crew and script, language barriers, frequent delays, unstable governments, riots, civil war, and less than adequate housing facilities for the cast and crew. Of course, some of these same problems may be experienced in Los Angeles.

The right amount of blocked funds. The producer will also have to find a company that has blocked funds in a given foreign country sufficient to meet the film production needs of the particular film.

Other costs. Unless the producer is able to conduct all of the necessary research, phone calls, inquiries, negotiations and documentation required to put together a blocked funds deal, the producer's representative and/or attorney will have to be compensated for conducting those activities on behalf of the producer.

Further Reading

"Creative Financing 1990: Myth vs. Reality." Michael Lewis and Robert Norton. *The Hollywood Reporter* (Entertainment Finance Special Report), p. F-34, August 1990.

Film and Video Financing. Michael Wiese. Michael Wiese Productions, 1991.

Film Finance and Distribution—A Dictionary of Terms. John W. Cones. Silman-James Press, 1992.

Film Industry Contracts. John W. Cones. Self-published, 1993.

"Information for Overseas Filmmakers—Australian Film and Television Information." Australian Film Commission, February 1992.

"Official AFCI Directory." Association of Film Commissioners International (Salt Lake City). *Locations Magazine*, Fall 1993.

37

Foreign Currency Deals

A so-called foreign currency deal is a film-financing arrangement in which a foreign country, for example, an eastern European nation, will offer to provide goods and production services for below-the-line costs for a small amount of so-called hard currency (U.S. dollars). Currencies may include anything that is in circulation in a given country as a medium of exchange, including coins, paper money, government notes and bank notes.

A currency conversion occurs when the money of one country is exchanged for an equivalent amount of another country's money. The measure of value of currencies traded between various countries is referred to as the exchange rate. An exchange rate is considered beneficial when the currency exchange rate favors a particular currency relative to the value of the currencies of other countries.

From time to time a country's currency relative to gold and/or the currencies of other nations will decline in value; thus, a devaluation of the local currency is said to have occurred. Devaluation can also result from a rise in value of other currencies relative to the currency of a particular country.

The countries that may offer foreign currency deals to filmmakers have most likely suffered recent or long-term downturns in the value of their currency. Producers interested in this strategy of film finance will want to identify international currency traders or international attorneys who may be able to assist in selecting countries that offer such exchanges.

Advantages

Possible increased production values. Foreign currency deals may permit the producer to leverage a smaller quantity of hard currency production dollars and to acquire an increased quantity of goods and services for the same amount of cash.

Combined with international coproductions. The foreign currency deal is another technique that may be combined with international coproductions to enhance the value of an internationally produced feature film.

Disadvantages

Potential problems. Aside from being rare, foreign currency deals, as with many film-financing arrangements involving foreign locations, typically mean that the film's producer will have to successfully negotiate through a difficult and archaic bureaucratic system, that the technical production expertise and equipment made available is not up to par, that living standards may be unacceptable to many of the film's above-the-line personnel and that extraordinary logistical problems are created.

Primary reason for utilizing the foreign currency deal. Producers who have experience with these sorts of arrangements suggest that in order to justify the use of this financing technique the desirability of the location must be a more important consideration for the particular film than saving money.

Further Reading

"Creative Financing 1990: Myth vs. Reality." Michael Lewis and Robert Norton. *The Hollywood Reporter* (Entertainment Finance Special Report), p. F-34, August 1990.

Film and Video Financing. Michael Wiese. Michael Wiese Productions, 1991.

Film Finance and Distribution—A Dictionary of Terms. John W. Cones. Silman-James Press, 1992.

Film Industry Contracts. John W. Cones. Self-published, 1993.

"Information for Overseas Filmmakers—Australian Film and Television Information." Australian Film Commission, February 1992.

"Official AFCI Directory." Association of Film Commissioners International (Salt Lake City). *Locations Magazine*, Fall 1993.

38

Foreign Below-the-Line or Facilities Deals

What the producers get. Some foreign governments, for example, Czechoslovakia, Poland and Russia, have offered to provide the crew, locations, local cast, studio facilities and cameras to cover approximately 70 percent of the film's below-the-line costs. In exchange, they usually ask for distribution rights in the eastern European countries and that a significant portion of the film be shot in the host country. Usually film stock is not included, and the cameras are not very good. Most U.S. productions utilizing below-the-line facilities deals have taken their own lighting (see "Official AFCI Directory" under Further Reading).

Relationship to coproduction deals. Some of the below-the-line or facilities deals are also considered international coproduction deals if foreign coproduction treaties are involved (see chapter 39).

Advantages

Reduced out-of-pocket costs. Since a significant portion of the below-the-line budget may be contributed in this manner, the producer does not have to come up with as much money to produce the film.

Greater value. The value of the below-the-line facilities offered may be more important to the producer than the film distribution rights given up.

Disadvantages

Sometimes an active partner. If a country provides more than 50 percent of the below the-line costs, it is likely to want to have some creative input; that is, it may become an active partner.

Production problems. Again, many of the problems typically associated with any foreign film production will also be encountered in a below-the-line facilities deal, namely, restrictive regulations relating to cast, crew and script, language barriers, frequent delays, unstable governments, riots, and civil war, less than adequate housing facilities for the cast and crew.

Further Reading

Feature Film Fund—Policies. Telefilm Canada, 1991–1992.

Film Finance and Distribution—A Dictionary of Terms. John W. Cones. Silman-James Press, 1992.

Film Industry Contracts. John W. Cones. Self-published, 1993.

"Information for Overseas Filmmakers—Australian Film and Television Information." Australian Film Commission, February 1992.

"Official AFCI Directory." Association of Film Commissioners International (Salt Lake City), *Locations Magazine*, Fall 1993.

"Producing a Film in Canada—The Legal and Regulatory Framework." David B. Zitzerman and Michael A. Levine. *The Entertainment and Sports Lawyer* 8, no. 4 (Winter 1991).

"Strategies for the International Production and Distribution of Feature Films in the 1990's." Thomas J. Cryan, David W. Johnson, James S. Crane, and Anthony Cammarata. *Loyola Entertainment Law Journal* 8 (1988).

39

International Coproductions

Regular coproductions. Generally speaking, feature film coproduction financing involves a sharing between two or more entities of the responsibilities relating to the financing of a film production. Distributor-financiers may make coproduction deals with one or more parties for one or more territories so that the risks associated with financing the production of the film will be spread among several parties. Numerous items relating to decision-making authority on various production questions must also be negotiated in order to avoid conflicts on such issues inherent in coproduction relationships.

International coproductions are more formal. International coproductions involve international coproduction treaties that exist between several countries, including Australia, the United Kingdom, Italy, France, Germany, Japan, China, Norway and Canada. In order to qualify as an international coproduction, the film must meet the requirements set out in one or more of the various treaties. If the film qualifies, it then may be eligible for several forms of financial support in the applicable countries, for example, tax benefits, government loans, government grants/subsidies and/or below-the-line/facilities deals. Such arrangements may also permit a U.S.-based producer to exceed television quotas in certain countries (since the film may then qualify as a local film).

The deal itself. International coproduction deals may simply divide territories between the coproducers or go so far as to split worldwide profits from the film or films based on some complex negotiated formula. The coproduction treaties themselves may require that the coproduction agreement set out the specific arrangements relating to the financial interest of each coproducer, the apportionment of the receipts generated by the film among the coproducers and the arrangements that have been made with respect to the respective liability of the coproducers.

Added value. The international coproduction may add value to

167

foreign rights. As an example, film rights presold in France might bring $1 million, $3–4 million if handled through the U.S.-based international distributor UIP, but as much as $10 million if the production is an international coproduction qualifying in France. Also, coproductions may help provide access to foreign subsidies (see discussion herein).

Qualification. Qualification for financial support offered through international coproduction treaties is difficult to obtain and requires that the film meet the test of *nationality* in each of the coproduction territories.

Tax status in the United States. Often the drafters of coproduction agreements will insert a provision that the agreement is governed by foreign law and that nothing in the agreement should be construed to indicate that a partnership or joint venture has been created between the coproducers. However, such statements do not determine the status of the transaction or entity for U.S. tax purposes when one of the coproducers is a U.S. producer. The IRS will determine whether the transaction has resulted in the creation of a taxable or nontaxable entity or whether it should be characterized as a loan (see chapter 10), an equity investment or merely presold film rights.

IRS characterization. On the one hand, the IRS will most likely characterize a coproduction arrangement that permits the coproducers to actively participate in the production and distribution of the film and share in the worldwide profits of the film as some form of entity, that is, a joint venture (sometimes referred to as an international coproduction partnership), a corporation or an association taxable as a corporation. On the other hand, the arrangement involving the sale of territorial rights to a foreign individual or entity in exchange for part of the production financing is more likely to be considered merely a foreign equity investment or presale in which no taxable entity has been created.

Tax treatment reminder. Joint ventures and limited partnerships are not taxed at the entity level; the corporations and associations taxable as corporations are taxed at the entity level. Producers seeking out coproduction opportunities should identify attorneys with international film coproduction expertise (including those whose articles appear under Further Reading).

Advantages

Access to other financing options. The international coproduction may help the producer to access other foreign finance options such as below-the-line deals or government subsidies.

Increased value. Film projects may be more valuable for some purposes in a local country if considered a local project.

Disadvantages

Withholding problems. A joint venture, limited partnership or international coproduction partnership (even though not a taxable entity in the United States) is obligated to pay quarterly estimated tax payments on behalf of the foreign coproducer partner, and both coproducers could be held liable for this obligation as withholding agents (IRS Code Section 1446). In addition, the IRS will probably treat such an entity as the employer of all personnel hired by either coproducer. This may make both coproducers liable for the entity's U.S. wage withholding obligations.

No U.S. treaties. The United States does not have formalized international coproduction treaties with other countries.

Added complexity. The international coproduction adds another layer of complexity to an already complex transaction and will inevitably require the expertise of an international attorney experienced in this particular form of film finance.

Further Reading

"Allure of Puerto Rico— Tax Breaks, Prod'n Fund Emphasized at Fest." Deborah Young. *Daily Variety*, p. 6, November 22, 1993.

"Creative Financing 1990: Myth vs. Reality." Michael Lewis and Robert Norton. *The Hollywood Reporter* (Entertainment Finance Special Report), p. F–34, August 1990.

Feature Film Fund—Policies. Telefilm Canada, 1991–1992.

Film Finance and Distribution—A Dictionary of Terms. John W. Cones. Silman-James Press, 1992.

Film Industry Contracts. John W. Cones. Self-published, 1993.

"Financing Film and Television Productions—Global Opportunities Emerging in the 1990's." Bruce St. J Lilliston. *Los Angeles Lawyer*, April 1990.

"Financing Independent Films—Wall Street Funding May be Drying Up, But New Opportunities Beckon from Europe and the Far East." Bruce St. J Lilliston. *Los Angeles Lawyer*, p. 19, May 1988.

"The Financing of Independent Motion Pictures in 1989." Peter J. Dekom. *American Premiere*, 1989.

"Foreign Productions and Foreign Financing—The Canadian Perspective."

Michael A. Levine and David B. Zitzerman. *The Entertainment and Sports Lawyer* 5, no. 4 (Spring 1987).

"The Last Emperor and Co-Producing in China: The Impossible Made Easy, and the Easy Made Impossible." Simon M. Olswang. *The Entertainment and Sports Lawyer* 6, no. 2 (Fall 1987).

"Official AFCI Directory." Association of Film Commissioners International (Salt Lake City), *Locations Magazine*, Fall 1993.

"Producing a Film in Canada—The Legal and Regulatory Framework." David B. Zitzerman and Michael A. Levine. *The Entertainment and Sports Lawyer* 8, no. 4 (Winter 1991).

"Strategies for the International Production and Distribution of Feature Films in the 1990's." Thomas J. Cryan, David W. Johnson, James S. Crane, and Anthony Cammarata. *Loyola Entertainment Law Journal*, 8 (1988).

"U.S./Foreign Film Funding (Co-Production Tips)." Nigel Sinclair. *Entertainment Law and Finance*, March 1991.

40

Foreign Tax Shelters and Incentives

Tax shelters defined. Generally speaking, a tax shelter is a transaction by means of which a taxpayer reduces his or her tax liability by engaging in activities that provide deductions or tax credits to apply against his or her tax liability. Thus, the tax shelter is a method used by investors to legally avoid or reduce tax liabilities. The specific tax benefits provided by the foreign motion picture tax shelters for foreign investors are (1) more rapid depreciation, which in some instances can be increased by borrowing, (2) deferral of income (tax deferral deals) and (3) conversion of ordinary income to capital gains, which is subject to a lower rate of tax.

General and specific laws. The tax laws of ten foreign countries, namely, France, Sweden, Britain (limited), Ireland, Germany, Spain, Canada, Australia, New Zealand and Japan, permit (and in some instances specifically encourage) motion picture tax shelters or tax-driven motion picture financing. The Canadian film tax shelter, for example, is the result of intentional tax subsidies for local film production. The German and Japanese motion picture tax shelters have been the unintended result of more general tax provisions.

Sweden and Canada. In recent years, Swedish laws have been structured so that if Swedish investors buy distribution rights in a film, that investment will be 100 percent deductible in the year of the investment. The Canadian tax shelter leverage is not as great as the leverage that was available in the mid-eighties in the United States, and in order for the investment to pay off, the Canadian films need to generate a profit.

Puerto Rico. Although not a foreign country, Puerto Rico also offers tax breaks for local film productions. The Puerto Rican government has passed new legislation that allows local investors to write off a portion of their investment while the film is still in production and permits some 80 to 90 percent of the film's revenues to remain tax exempt after the picture begins recouping its costs (see article cited in Further Reading).

Advantages

Investor interest. Investors may be more inclined to invest if significant tax benefits are available.

Specialized assistance available. Law and accounting firms with expertise in international tax shelters and tax incentives are available to assist in structuring film finance opportunities utilizing such techniques.

Disadvantages

Changing tax laws. The tax laws of each country change from time to time; therefore, it is difficult to keep current on those laws unless you specialize in this form of film finance. Some of the information in this summary may have become obsolete during the time in which this book was being prepared for publication.

Professional help. Most producers will almost certainly require the assistance of a professional accountant or attorney who specializes in international tax law in order to properly structure a tax-sheltered deal for another country.

Further Reading

"Allure of Puerto Rico—Tax Breaks, Prod'n Fund Emphasized at Fest." Deborah Young. *Daily Variety*, p. 6, November 22, 1993.

"Creative Financing 1990: Myth vs. Reality." Michael Lewis and Robert Norton. *The Hollywood Reporter* (Entertainment Finance Special Report), p. F-34, August 1990.

Film Finance and Distribution—A Dictionary of Terms. John W. Cones. Silman-James Press, 1992.

Film Industry Contracts. John W. Cones. Self-published, 1993.

"Foreign Productions and Foreign Financing—The Canadian Perspective." Michael A. Levine and David B. Zitzerman. *The Entertainment and Sports Lawyer* 5, no. 4 (Spring 1987).

International Tax Planning Manual. Commerce Clearing House (updated periodically).

"Jamaica Tax Break Boon for Prod'n." Duane Byrge. *The Hollywood Reporter*, October 18, 1991.

"Official AFCI Directory." Association of Film Commissioners International (Salt Lake City), *Locations Magazine*, Fall 1993.

"Producing a Film in Canada—The Legal and Regulatory Framework." David B. Zitzerman and Michael A. Levine. *The Entertainment and Sports Lawyer* 8, no. 4 (Winter 1991).

"Strategies for the International Production and Distribution of Feature Films in the 1990's." Thomas J. Cryan, David W. Johnson, James S. Crane and Anthony Cammarata. *Loyola Entertainment Law Journal* 8 (1988).

Tax Shelters—The Basics. Arthur Andersen and Co., Harper and Row, 1982.

Tax Shelters—The Botton Line. Robert A. Stanger, 1982.

41

Foreign Government Grants or Subsidies

Foreign government grants are specific donations by foreign governments to filmmakers to assist in the production of a film that is deemed advantageous to the country or a given locale within the country that is served by that government. In other words, production of the movie will provide jobs and help the economy in a given area, or the movie will provide favorable publicity for the locale. As an example, government-approved films in Austria receive 80 percent of the budget from that country's government, leaving the producer responsible for the 20 percent balance.

Information relating to foreign subsidy film programs is available through each country's embassies or film commissions (see "Official AFCI Directory" under Further Reading). In all likelihood, it would be helpful to have a coproducer associated with the film project seeking funding who is a citizen and resident of the country from which the grant is being sought.

Advantages

The right movie. The right movie can obtain significant financial assistance in this manner.

International coproductions. A producer's chances of obtaining a foreign government grant may be increased if the production qualifies as a coproduction in the country from which the grant is being sought.

Disadvantages

Subsidies. Foreign film subsidies granted by foreign governments usually require that most of the film be shot in the subsidizing country, using almost exclusively native technicians, facilities and actors.

Staff expertise. A producer seeking to utilize such film finance techniques (or someone else on the producer's staff, the production

174

attorney or a consultant on the picture) has to become very familiar with the foreign regulatiᵒns governing such subsidies and the production of the film.

Limited funds. Onlʏ limited funds can be accessed in this manner.

Further Reading

"Creative Financing 1990ː Myth vs. Reality." Michael Lewis and Robert Norton. *The Hollywoodʹ Reporter* (Entertainment Finance Special Report), p. F-34, August 1990.

Film Finance and Distrib ution—A Dictionary of Terms. John W. Cones. Silman-James Press, 1992.

Film Industry Contracts. John W. Cones. Self-published, 1993.

"Finding a Formula to Fiⁿance Indies. Scott Young. *The Hollywood Reporter*, January 25, 1991.

"Foreign Productions and ʾoreign Financing—The Canadian Perspective." Michael A. Levine and David B. Zitzerman. *The Entertainment and Sports Lawyer* 5, no. 4 (Spring 1987).

International Tax Handbook. Horwath International, 1993.

"Official AFCI Directory." Association of Film Commissioners International (Salt Lake City), *Locatᵒons Magazine*, Fall 1993.

"Producing a Film in Caⁿada—The Legal and Regulatory Framework." David B. Zitzerman and Michael A. Levine. *The Entertainment and Sports Lawyer* 8, no. 4 (Winter 1991).

"Strategies for the Interⁿational Production and Distribution of Feature Films in the 1990's." Thomas J. Cryan, David W. Johnson, James S. Crane, and Anthony Cⁱmmarata. *Loyola Entertainment Law Journal* 8 (1988).

42

Foreign Debt Capitalization Programs

Formal programs. Quite a few third-world countries owe large amounts of money to foreign banks, and those countries have adopted so-called debt capitalization programs in an effort to encourage the purchase of the foreign country's debt at a significant discount and its exchange for foreign currency to be used for production activities in the foreign country. The discounts typically range from 40 to 60 percent. The debt will be exchanged for its full face amount in the foreign currency. Countries with debt capitalization programs include Mexico, Brazil, Costa Rica and the Philippines.

How to proceed. The producer with a motion picture that can be shot on location in a foreign country and who desires to consider using a debt capitalization program should first contact the U.S. office of a representative of that foreign country and inquire as to the existence of a debt capitalization program (see "Official AFCI Directory" under Further Reading). If such a program is in effect, the producer will have to complete an application that must then be approved by the foreign country. Once approved, the foreign currency is contributed to a corporation incorporated in that foreign country, the stock of which is owned by the U.S. producer. The foreign corporation then produces the film in the foreign country. The completed motion picture is actually owned by the foreign corporation, but it can be licensed back to the U.S. producer. In some instances, it is possible for all ownership rights to remain with the U.S. producer.

Possible unfavorable tax consequences. Depending on the country involved, the specific manner in which the transaction is structured and the way the U.S. production company conducts its activities, unfavorable tax consequences may arise from a debt capitalization program; for example, income to the U.S. producer may be recognized immediately when the purchased debt is converted into the foreign currency. Also, in some cases, foreign tax may be imposed on income earned on the motion picture. Thus, the advice of an international tax attc rney or accountant should be sought in structuring this sort of film fi nance transaction.

Advantages

Economic conseque. ices. The producer is reducing third-world debt while also making a film and contributing to the local economy.

Discounted funds. Moneys are available at significant discounts.

Limited partnership combination. Plans to take advantage of a specific foreign debt cap italization program may prove to be an effective selling point to prospective limited partnership investors since their money can then be leveraged to purchase significantly greater production values.

Disadvantages

Specialized expertise. Generally speaking, the services of someone who has expertise n this area of finance will be required. The Debt-for-Development Coalition, based in Washington, D.C., provides consulting service s relating to debt capitalization programs (see listing under Further Reading).

Takes money to get money. The third-world debt has to be purchased; thus, some leve of up front funding is required.

Further Reading

Film Finance and Distribution—A Dictionary of Terms. John W. Cones. Silman-James Press, 1992.

Film Industry Contracts. John W. Cones. Self-published, 1993.

"Official AFCI Directory." Association of Film Commissioners International (Salt Lake City), *Locations Magazine*, Fall 1993.

"A Shot in the Arm for Film Financing—Collaborative Effort Seeks International Debt Swap." Carol U. Ozemhoya. *South Florida Business Journal*, April 20, 1992.

"Strategies for the International Production and Distribution of Feature Films in the 1990's." Thomas J. Cryan, David W. Johnson, James S. Crane, and Anthony Cammarata. *Loyola Entertainment Law Journal* 8 (1988).

"What is Debt-for-Development?" The Debt-for-Development Coalition (Washington, D.C.), April 18, 1991.

43

Foreign-Equity Financing

Profit participation. Foreign-equity financing involves film funding provided by foreign sources (non-U.S.) in exchange for an ownership interest or profit participation in the film or films financed or in the entity producing such film(s). In addition to requiring an equity participation in the film's receipts, foreign equity investors typically demand that certain territories be reserved for them.

Equity interest in entity. Foreign-equity financing could also involve raising money by offering equity ownership interests in the production entity, for example, shares of common or preferred stock for a corporate production company or limited partnership interests in a limited partnership. Equity financing of a feature film enables the producer to finance the film unhampered by studio executives and the pitfalls of studio financing.

Advantages

Local guidance. When the foreign partners are industry insiders in their home market, they often can provide expertise in exploiting the film or films in that territory and in guiding a particular film production through complex governmental bureaucracy.

Local favorites. Movies that are considered partly domestic productions in foreign countries may be accorded some favoritism when foreign partners are aboard.

Disadvantages

Creative control. Depending on the arrangements, the foreign equity investor becomes the financial and/or creative partner of the domestic producer.

Foreign currency. These transactions will require some knowledge of the current value of foreign currencies with the attendant risk of such values falling or rising unpredictably.

Further Reading

"Black-Belt Yen Men Girl for Lean Times—Pipeline to Hollywood Running Dry." Garth Alexander. *Variety*, September 21, 1992.

"Creative Financing 1990: Myth vs. Reality." Michael Lewis and Robert Norton. *The Hollywood Reporter* (Entertainment Finance Special Report), p. F-34, August 1990.

Film and Video Financing. Michael Wiese. Michael Wiese Productions, 1991.

The Film Entertainment Industry. Schuyler M. Moore. Commerce Clearing House Tax Transactions Library (updated periodically).

Film Finance and Distribution—A Dictionary of Terms. John W. Cones. Silman-James Press, 1992.

Film Industry Contracts. John W. Cones. Self-published, 1993.

"Foreign Affairs." Nigel Sinclair and Michael Yanover. *Daily Variety*, June 26, 1991.

"Foreign Productions and Foreign Financing—The Canadian Perspective." Michael A. Levine and David B. Zitzerman. *The Entertainment and Sports Lawyer* 5, no. 4 (Spring 1987).

"Hollywood Goes Boffo Overseas." Alan Citron. *Los Angeles Times*, March 30, 1992.

Independent Feature Film Production—A Complete Guide from Concept to Distribution. Gregory Goodell. St. Martin's Press, 1982.

"Japanese Investors Cooling to Lure of Hollywood, Confab Told." Robert Marich. *The Hollywood Reporter*, p. 14, June 17, 1991.

"Official AFCI Directory," Association of Film Commissioners International (Salt Lake City), *Locations Magazine*, Fall 1993.

"Producing a Film in Canada—The Legal and Regulatory Framework." David B. Zitzerman and Michael A. Levine. *The Entertainment and Sports Lawyer* 8, no. 4 (Winter 1991).

"Strategies for the International Production and Distribution of Feature Films in the 1990's." Thomas J. Cryan, David W. Johnson, James S. Crane, and Anthony Cammarata. *Loyola Entertainment Law Journal* 8 (1988).

INDEX

INDEX

Index

John W. Cone s is a securities and entertainment attorney based in Los Angeles, where he maintains a private solo practice advising independent feature film, video, television and theatrical producer clients. A frequent lecturer on film finance and distribution, his lectures on "Investor Financing of Entertainment Projects" have been presented in Los Angeles, Las Vegas, Dallas, Houston, Boise, Sacramento, Portland and San Francisco and were sponsored by the American Film Institute state film commissions and independent producer organizations. He has also lectured for the USC Cinema-TV School, the UCLA (graduate level) Producer's Program, the UCLA Extension and the UCLA Anderson Graduate School of Management. His previous publications include *Film Finance and Distribution—A Dictionary of Terms*, *Film Industry Contracts* and numerous magazine and journal articles.